GET WAISTED

100 Addictively Delicious Plant-Based Entrées

MARY WENDT, MD AND TESS CHALLIS

DOCTOR DOCTOR PRESS

Contents

Lean Beans

Power Pasta

Radiant Rice

Gorgeous Grains

Slimming Soups

Wraps and Sammies

What do you eat for dinner?

If you're like most Americans, you choose meat, accompanied by a potato or grain and a vegetable. These are probably the choices most of your neighbors and friends are eating, and are similar to the favorite foods that your parents fed you when you were growing up. You may be surprised to find yourself in the shape you're in, carrying a little extra weight or swallowing pills each morning, despite your best efforts at doing the right thing. You might be just like me.

Six years ago, despite regular exercise and plenty of sleep, I was diagnosed with pre-diabetes and elevated cholesterol. I took an honest look at my supposedly healthy diet, and suggested some changes to my doctor. However, he didn't think diet had any impact on disease. Despite his opinion, I changed my diet and cured my conditions! Maybe you have asked your doctor about weight loss, like the two-thirds of U.S. adults that are overweight or obese (1). Unfortunately, if you are asking your doctor for advice about nutrition, chances are you already know more than your doctor (2).

If you were to get a sunburn, you wouldn't cover it with makeup and continue sun exposure. Too often, that is exactly what the medical establishment does. Medicine doesn't treat the causes of disease, it treats the effects. Hypertension, diabetes, and high cholesterol get their separate pills, with the focus remaining on treating the symptoms instead of the whole of the problem. Despite the array of pills we have at our disposal and the exorbitantly high costs of health care, Americans are not any healthier.

Medicine is terrific at managing trauma and acute surgical conditions like appendicitis, but the rates of chronic diseases like obesity, diabetes, and hypertension are only increasing over time. Nutrition and lifestyle change the expression of genes that cause health or disease outcomes, by turning on healthy genes or suppressing diseased genes. Of course, no diet can repair a broken neck. Within the realm of lifestyle modification, however, nutrition plays the biggest role in gene expression, over sleep, relationships and exercise.

Personally, I do find some foods irresistible, which is exactly the way the highly profitable processed food industry wants it. Farmers get very little of our food dollars today; most of the profit in food is going to large food processors and restaurants that layer whole foods with sugars, salt and fats to make them too good to be true. If you find yourself dreaming about foods that you know are not good for you, you are certainly not alone. Addiction to food means that despite knowing it is bad for you and knowing that you don't need it, you keep eating anyway. Addiction means that the craving is controlling your behavior toward the food, instead of you being in control.

When women with high addiction testing scores drink a chocolate milkshake, our brains show the same reaction of drug addicts when they anticipate using. The sugary, fatty foods trigger the same areas of the brain that respond to sex, drugs and gambling. (3) However, you can reset your addictive centers in your brain to desire the delicious, nutritious, healing foods like the ones in this book.

Every day I hear grateful testimonials about the healing power of whole, plant-based foods that I've prescribed to my patients. The overall power of their combined experience is substantial, even if 400 large nutritional studies didn't already prove the healing power of whole, plant-based foods. You have probably heard that eating whole, plant-based foods results in a decreased risk for cancer (4), Alzheimer disease (5), and heart disease (6).

Avoiding meat is also associated with a nice reduction in body weight. The average vegan is 40 pounds lighter than the average American (7). Good nutrition reduces disease, increases energy levels, restores ideal body weight, preserves the environment, and slows global warming. We are used to prescription drugs having a long list of potential side effects that are seemingly unrelated to the primary indication for the drug. With nutrition, we can prescribe an intervention that will treat the root cause of disease, with side effects we can actually enjoy.

We truly can change the course of our health and our planet, just by changing our dinner.

Dr. Mary

1. Flegal et al, JAMA, 303(3):235-241, 2010
2. Lazarus et al, Nutrition knowledge and practices of physicians in a family-practice residency program: the effect of an education program provided by a physician nutrition specialist, Am J Clin Nutr September 1993 vol. 58 no. 3 319-325
3. Gearhardt et al, The Neural Correlates of Food Addiction, Arch Gen Psychiatry. 2011;68(8):808-816.
4. http://preventcancer.aicr.org
5. Morris, M. C. et al, Dietary Fats and the Risk of Incident Alzheimer Disease. Arch. Neurol. 60:194-200, 2003.
6. Crowe, et al, Risk of Hospitalization or Death From Ischemic Heart Disease Among British Vegetarians and Non-Vegetarians: Results from the EPIC-Oxford Cohort Study, First published January 30, 2013, doi: 10.3945/ajcn .112.044073
7. Tonstad et al, Type of Vegetarian Diet, Body Weight, and Prevalence of Type 2 Diabetes, Diabetes Care. 2009 May; 32(5): 791–796.

Tess Challis is an author, vegan chef, and wellness coach..

She spent many hours in her kitchen creating these recipes for you and hopes they'll make your life easier, healthier, and even more delicious!

Tess began her holistic health journey in her late teens. After a lifetime of numerous health ailments (including severe acne, obesity, constant illnesses, anxiety, and depression), she found that a vegan diet along with an inner wellness regime made all the difference.

In 1994, she began to work as a personal chef across the country. In 2008, Tess shifted her focus to writing, coaching, speaking, and teaching healthy plant-based cooking. She continues to speak and teach across the country. Empowering others to get healthy in their own homes and kitchens is one of Tess's greatest passions. She believes that food should not only be supremely healthy, but also completely satisfying and flavorful—why not have it all?

Her previous books include **Radiant Health, Inner Wealth, The Two-Week Wellness Solution** (foreword by Dr. Neal Barnard), and **Radiance 4 Life** (foreword by Robert Cheeke). She is currently working on three more books as well as the **Get Waisted** health and weight loss program along with Dr. Mary.

Tess is the proud mama of a healthy ten-year-old vegan girl.

In the next few chapters,

you'll find a variety of easy to make plant-based main dishes—everything from light and filling bean dishes to crowd-pleasing pasta favorites. These recipes have been created to do two very important things—both satisfy your palate with delicious flavors and also keep you trim and healthy. You'll soon find that you don't need to sacrifice great taste for nutrition. Your journey to health really can be one that's filled with satisfaction!

To further ensure your success, we've color-coded our recipes. Color codes are an easy, fun way to make sure you're eating in balance. If you're wanting to lose weight quickly, you'll find that basing your diet on "Green" recipes will get you to your goals quickly. However, a few slightly richer "Blue" recipes thrown in occasionally can give you that feeling of indulging, yet without doing anything too crazy! As a general rule for weight loss, eat up to one serving of a "Blue" dish per day but base your diet on "Green" recipes— and don't forget to include plenty of fresh veggies!

Here's your color code cheat sheet:

Green: "Green" recipes are low in fat and calories, yet high in nutrients. Emphasize them in your quest for weight loss and optimal health.

Blue: "Blue" recipes are slightly higher in plant-based fats and/or sugars. They're best eaten in moderation (up to one serving per day) if you're wanting to lose weight quickly.

Nutritional information prepared by www.menutrinfo.com.

Visit DrMaryMD.com for more detailed recipe information.

Welcome and
GET WAISTED!

Lean Beans

Do you have any idea how freaking amazing beans are? The seemingly humble bean is a powerhouse of fiber, iron, and minerals. Not only that, beans have just as much protein as meat and are very low in fat, extremely filling, and endlessly versatile. In other words, beans are your new best friend—they'll keep you slim, satisfied, and vibrantly healthy!

Ever So Nice Beans N Rice

This dish is hearty, filling, and flavorful. For an extra kick, feel free to add your favorite hot sauce!

Three 15 oz. cans black beans
2 teaspoons EACH: dried oregano, "Chicky Baby Seasoning" (p. 16), and ground cumin
2 large bay leaves
1 large onion, diced
2 fresh tomatoes, diced
1 tablespoon balsamic vinegar

Rice:
1 cup long grain brown rice
2 cups water
2 tablespoons "Chicky Baby Seasoning"

Final Freshness:
2 tablespoons EACH: fresh lemon juice and minced cilantro
5 medium cloves garlic, minced or pressed
Sea salt, to taste

In a large pot, combine the beans, oregano, Chicky Baby, cumin, bay leaves, onion, tomatoes, and balsamic vinegar. Bring to a boil over high heat. Reduce the heat to low and simmer, uncovered, for about 45 minutes. You'll want to stir this every 15 minutes or so while it's cooking.

While the beans are doing their deal, rice it up. If you have a rice cooker, this will be profoundly simple. If not, it will be really simple. Just place the rice, water, and seasoning in a covered pot and stir well. Bring to a boil over high heat. Reduce heat to low and simmer, covered the whole time, until the rice has absorbed all of the water. This should time out rather perfectly with the beans.

Once the beans are done, stir in the lemon juice, cilantro, garlic, and salt. Serve over the cooked rice. If you like, garnish with additional cilantro, diced onion, lemon wedges, and hot sauce.

Serves 6/GF/SF/Green

Calories	Saturated fat (g)	Poly unsat fat (g)	Mono unsat fat (g)	Cholesterol (mg)	Sodium (mg)	Potassium (mg)	Carbohydrate (g)	Dietary fiber (g)	Sugars (g)	Protein (g)
347	0.4	0.7	0.5	0	1114	949	66	17.7	3.1	17.6

Chicky Baby Seasoning

This all-purpose "chicken" flavoring puts an end to expensive store-bought seasonings—plus it's so much healthier! You can also use it to make "chicken" broth (use one tablespoon of this mix per cup of water). It's especially delicious in soups, gravies, and rice pilaf—yum!

- 1 cup nutritional yeast powder
- 3 tablespoons EACH: dried onion granules and seasoned salt
- 2 teaspoons EACH: celery seed and dried garlic granules
- 2 tablespoons dried parsley flakes
- ½ teaspoon EACH: ground black pepper and white pepper
- 1 teaspoon EACH: lemon pepper, sugar, dried dill, and dried rosemary

Combine all of the ingredients with a whisk or spoon until well mixed. Store in an airtight container out of direct sunlight. This will keep for several months.

Makes about 1½ cups/GF/SF/Green

Thai Green Curry Hummus

This is like all the flavors of a delicious Thai meal in one delicious dip. Serve this with baked whole grain pita crisps (or bread) and assorted raw veggies for a fun, snacky entrée!

- 2 cups chickpeas, cooked and drained
- ¼ cup plus 2 tablespoons fresh lime juice
- ¼ cup coconut oil
- ¼ cup fresh basil
- ¼ cup water
- 2 teaspoons green curry paste (such as Thai Kitchen brand)
- 1 teaspoon sea salt

Place all of the ingredients in a food processor or blender.

Blend until thoroughly combined, smooth, and creamy. This will keep for about one week, refrigerated in an airtight container.

Serves 4/GF/SF/Blue

	Calories	Saturated fat (g)	Poly unsat fat (g)	Mono unsat fat (g)	Cholesterol (mg)	Sodium (mg)	Potassium (mg)	Carbohydrate (g)	Dietary fiber (g)	Sugars (g)	Protein (g)
CBS	26	0	0	0	0	591	127	3	1.6	.3	3.2
TGCH	261	12	1.2	1.3	0	692	273	25	6.9	4.3	7.4

Savory Soul Bowl

For when you want everything good and comforting in one bowl.

One recipe Feel Good Mac N Cheese (p. 61)
One recipe BBQ Tempeh (p. 135)
2 cans black-eyed peas, drained and rinsed

King Kale:
1 lb. (4 cups packed) lacinato kale ribbons, washed well
¼ cup liquid vegetarian broth
2 teaspoons oil (coconut, olive, or sunflower)
4 medium cloves garlic, minced or pressed
4 teaspoons tamari
4 teaspoons fresh lemon juice
2 teaspoons nutritional yeast powder

1. Prepare the Mac N Cheese and BBQ tempeh and set aside.

2. Place the black-eyed peas in a medium pot and season to taste with a little sea salt. Stir and heat gently until warmed. Set aside.

3. To make the kale: Place the kale on a cutting board and cut off the thickest portion of the stem base. I don't remove the stems above this point, as they are tender enough to eat when cooked (if finely chopped). Cut the kale into thin ribbons. Place the kale along with the broth, oil, garlic, and tamari into a medium-large skillet. Cook over medium-high heat for about 5 minutes, stirring often, until bright green. Remove from heat. Toss with two teaspoons of the lemon juice and the nutritional yeast powder.

4. To assemble your bowls: scoop some pasta into each bowl. Place some beans and kale on the side and then dole out the tempeh. Now it's time to relax and have some good eats!

Serves 4-6/GF (if using gluten-free pasta)/Blue

Calories	Saturated fat (g)	Poly unsat fat (g)	Mono unsat fat (g)	Cholesterol (mg)	Sodium (mg)	Potassium (mg)	Carbohydrate (g)	Dietary fiber (g)	Sugars (g)	Protein (g)
623	7.7	2.7	2	0	1791	1100	95	13	12	28.7

Easy Indian Mung Beans

As the name implies, this recipe makes for a very easy and simple main dish. However, it's also yummy, satisfying, and one of those rare Indian dishes that's still delicious despite being so low in fat! Mung beans are khaki green in color, small, and cook more quickly than many other types of legumes. They're also easy to digest and very high in fiber.

1 cup dry mung beans, rinsed and drained
1 tablespoon grated fresh ginger
1 tablespoon coconut oil
1½ teaspoons EACH: cumin seeds and ground (dried) coriander
½ jalapeno, stem and seeds removed and diced
3 cups water
1¼ teaspoons sea salt
2 tablespoons lemon juice
½ cup fresh cilantro, chopped

Place the beans, ginger, oil, cumin seeds, coriander, jalapeno, and water in a large pot with a tight fitting lid (or a pressure cooker). Bring to a boil (covered) over high heat. Reduce the heat to low and simmer for about 45 minutes to an hour, or until the beans are tender. If you are using a pressure cooker, this will instead take about 20 minutes.

When the beans are tender, stir in the sea salt and fresh lemon juice. Garnish with fresh cilantro and serve.

Serves about 4/GF/SF/Green

5 Minute Chicky Chickpeas

This dish is perfect for when you need a healthy, filling dish in a hurry. It can be served over whole grain pasta, brown rice, or even a baked potato.

15 oz. can chickpeas, drained and rinsed (1½ cups cooked chickpeas)
¾ cup plain unsweetened nondairy milk
2 tablespoons nutritional yeast
1 tablespoon Chicky Baby Seasoning (p. 16)
2 teaspoons extra-virgin olive oil
2 large cloves garlic, minced or pressed
½ teaspoon dried rosemary
¼ teaspoon EACH: sea salt and black pepper

1. In a medium skillet, place the chickpeas. With a potato masher, smoosh them up a bit. You'll want to leave plenty of texture, while breaking up the whole chickpeas into bits.

2. Stir in the remaining ingredients. Bring to a boil, stirring often. Reduce heat to low and simmer until thickened, about 3-4 minutes. Serve warm, over whole grain pasta, brown rice, baked potatoes, or any other whole grain or vegetable.

Serves 2/GF/SF/Green

	Calories	Saturated fat (g)	Poly unsat fat (g)	Mono unsat fat (g)	Cholesterol (mg)	Sodium (mg)	Potassium (mg)	Carbohydrate (g)	Dietary fiber (g)	Sugars (g)	Protein (g)
EIMB	90	3	0.2	0.4	0	709	190	11.2	4.1	1.3	3.9
5MCC	469	1.5	3	4.6	0	656	978	65	19.7	10.7	28

Bean, Rice, and Veggie Bowl with Green Chili Lime Sauce

This dish is easy peasy to put together if you have cooked rice and beans on hand. Plus, it has pretty much everything–crunchy veggies, punchy flavor, immune-boosting ingredients, and hearty protein. Yeah baby!

3 cups cooked brown rice, warm
1½ cups cooked black beans
3 cups baby spinach
¾ cup EACH: chopped red cabbage and grated carrot
¼ – ½ cup minced onion (depending on your tolerance for raw onion)
1 small avocado, peeled and diced
¼ cup minced cilantro

Green Chili Lime Sauce
1 teaspoon olive oil
1 tablespoon flour (rice or whole wheat pastry)
One 13 oz. container (about 1½ cups) roasted, peeled, chopped mild green chilies, thawed if frozen
¼ cup fresh lime juice
1 teaspoon sea salt
5 medium cloves garlic, minced or pressed

Prepare your rice, beans, and veggies and set them aside. The sauce will come together quickly.

To make the sauce: Place the olive oil and flour in a medium pot set to medium heat. Stir well. Add the green chilies and stir with the oil/flour mixture until thoroughly combined. Cook for about 4 minutes, stirring occasionally, until it's a bit thicker. Turn off the heat. Add the remaining ingredients and stir well.

Place the spinach in the bottom of three large bowls. Add the beans and veggies (all except the avocado). Top each bowl evenly with the chili sauce. Garnish with avocado and cilantro and serve.

Serves 3/GF/SF/Green

Calories	Saturated fat (g)	Poly unsat fat (g)	Mono unsat fat (g)	Cholesterol (mg)	Sodium (mg)	Potassium (mg)	Carbohydrate (g)	Dietary fiber (g)	Sugars (g)	Protein (g)
554	2.2	2.4	8.3	0	813	1580	96	20	10.1	18.3

Tostada Bar

This is the perfect answer to "How do I feed my family in a way that works for all of us—me included?" When the toppings are presented buffet-style, everyone feels like they have a choice and can make up the perfect tostada, just for them!

Two 15 oz. cans vegetarian refried beans
2 teaspoons EACH: dried onion granules and cumin powder
4 medium cloves fresh garlic, minced or pressed
1 teaspoon EACH: seasoned salt and ground paprika
2 tablespoons fresh lime juice
8 corn tortillas

Toppings:
½ cup EACH: chopped tomato, chopped fresh cilantro, shredded carrots, red cabbage (grated or chopped), and minced red onion
Fresh salsa or hot sauce, to taste
One avocado, diced (or ½ cup guacamole)
8 lime wedges

Preheat the oven to 400° F. Place the corn tortillas on lightly oiled cookie sheets in a single layer. Spray (or brush) the tops of the tortillas very lightly with oil and bake for about 10 minutes, or until crisp and lightly browned. Remove from the oven and set aside.

Place the beans in a medium pot over low heat. Stir in the onion granules, cumin, garlic, seasoned salt, paprika, and 2 tablespoons lime juice. Cook, stirring often, until hot. Remove from heat.

Prepare the toppings and place them in individual bowls for maximum buffet cuteness.

To serve: Place some of the beans on each tortilla and spread out. Add the toppings of your choice and squeeze a lime wedge over the top. Serve immediately.

Serves 4-8/GF/SF/Green

21

Calories	Saturated fat (g)	Poly unsat fat (g)	Mono unsat fat (g)	Cholesterol (mg)	Sodium (mg)	Potassium (mg)	Carbohydrate (g)	Dietary fiber (g)	Sugars (g)	Protein (g)
254	1.1	1.7	3.9	0	889	856	39.9	12	3.3	10.6

Hungarian Chickpeas

Welcome to one of my ultimate obsessions.

  15 oz. can chickpeas (garbanzo beans), rinsed
    and drained
  2 tablespoons pitted and quartered kalamata
    olives (or other Greek olives)
  2 tablespoons EACH: raisins, chopped
    cilantro, and minced yellow or white onion
  1 tablespoon EACH: extra-virgin olive oil and
    raw agave nectar
  2 teaspoons EACH: dijon mustard, fresh lime
    juice, and smoked paprika
  1 teaspoon dried oregano
  2 large cloves garlic, minced or pressed
  ½ teaspoon sea salt

Combine all of the ingredients and stir very well.
Serve cold or at room temperature. This will keep,
refrigerated in an airtight container, for up to a week.

Serves 2/GF/SF/Green

	Calories	Saturated fat (g)	Poly unsat fat (g)	Mono unsat fat (g)	Cholesterol (mg)	Sodium (mg)	Potassium (mg)	Carbohydrate (g)	Dietary fiber (g)	Sugars (g)	Protein (g)
HC	501	1.7	3.4	6.3	0	759	789	79	18.1	25.1	20
SICF	510	4.8	2.6	1.8	0	1030	701	82	14.7	9.5	21

Spicy Indian Chickpea Fritters

These addictive little treats are the perfect way to satisfy your craving for something spicy, healthy, and flavorful!

One 15 oz. can chickpeas (garbanzo beans), drained and rinsed (1½ cups cooked chickpeas)
1 cup cooked quinoa
1 cup bread crumbs (whirl sprouted grain bread in a food processor until fine)
2 tablespoons fresh lemon juice
4-5 large cloves garlic, minced or pressed
1 tablespoon cumin seeds
2 teaspoons ground coriander
1 teaspoon EACH: sea salt and ground turmeric
½ teaspoon asafetida
¼ teaspoon ground cayenne

For pan-frying: 1 tablespoon oil (coconut or sunflower)

1. In a medium-large bowl, place the chickpeas. Mash well with a potato masher.

2. Stir in the quinoa, bread crumbs, lemon juice, garlic, cumin, coriander, salt, turmeric, asafetida, and cayenne. Combine thoroughly with a large spoon and set aside.

3. In a large skillet, heat one teaspoon of the oil over medium heat. Form the chickpea mixture into small patties and place them on the skillet. Cook for about 4 minutes on each side (turning over once), until both sides are golden-browned.

4. Continue to cook the fritters in batches, using the rest of the oil if needed, and serve warm.

Serves 3/GF/SF/Green

23

Black Bean, Cilantro, and Apricot Salad

This is a hearty (yet light) salad that can function either as a main dish or side. It is aesthetically beautiful and has an unusual, yet very appealing, blend of flavors. Although it needs to be marinated for several hours, the actual preparation time is under thirty minutes.

15 oz. can of black beans, drained and rinsed (1½ cups cooked beans)
½ cup EACH: chopped dried apricots, mango juice, and chopped cilantro
¼ cup EACH: diced carrots and corn kernels
2 scallions (green onions), trimmed and finely chopped
2 medium-large cloves garlic, minced or pressed
2 tablespoons EACH: olive oil (or other oil of choice) and fresh lime juice
½ tablespoon EACH: tamari (or shoyu or soy sauce) and grated fresh ginger
¾ teaspoon sea salt

Add Last: 4 cups (lightly packed) chopped baby spinach

Mix all of the ingredients (except for the spinach) together very well and place in an airtight container. Marinate for several hours or overnight in the refrigerator. While it is marinating, stir the mixture several times to make sure all of the ingredients get to know each other really well. Intimately.

Bring the salad to room temperature and toss with the spinach. Serve and savor the goodness.

Serves 4/GF/Green

Zesty Lemon Chickpeas

This fresh, lively dish is so delicious you'll forget how nutrient-dense and light it is!

One 15 oz. can chickpeas (garbanzo beans), drained (1½ cups cooked chickpeas)
¼ cup finely chopped parsley
2 tablespoons fresh lemon juice
2 teaspoons extra-virgin olive oil
1 teaspoon EACH: Dijon mustard and minced lemon zest
¼ teaspoon EACH: sea salt and black pepper
2 large cloves garlic, minced or pressed

In a large bowl, toss all of the ingredients. Gently stir well until thoroughly combined.

Serve cold or at room temperature.

Serves 2/GF/SF/Green

Lowfat Supercharged Hummus

This delicious hummus is much lower in fat (and higher in nutrients) than traditional hummus, so feel free to live it up! This makes for a great snacky meal along with some whole grain bread or tortillas, fresh vegetables, grape leaves, and vegan Greek salad. Yum!

One 15 oz. can garbanzo beans
¼ cup plus 1 tablespoon fresh lemon juice
2 tablespoons nutritional yeast
1 tablespoon EACH: mellow white miso and extra-virgin olive oil
3 large cloves garlic, peeled
½ teaspoon sea salt

Pour off all but ¼ cup of the bean liquid so that the beans are drained and you have ¼ cup liquid set aside.
Place all of the ingredients (including the ¼ cup bean liquid) in a good blender or food processor. Blend until very smooth and emulsified. This will store for several days, refrigerated in an airtight container.

Serves 4/GF/Green

	Calories	Saturated fat (g)	Poly unsat fat (g)	Mono unsat fat (g)	Cholesterol (mg)	Sodium (mg)	Potassium (mg)	Carbohydrate (g)	Dietary fiber (g)	Sugars (g)	Protein (g)
BBCAS	284	1.1	1.1	5	0	583	827	45.5	11.9	14.5	11.7
ZLC	403	1.3	3	4.6	0	360	696	61	16.7	10.7	19.4
LSH	236	0.8	1.8	3.2	0	451	431	33.9	9.4	5.9	12.4

Creamy Adzuki Beans

How often do you hear a resounding response of "yummm!" when serving up a pot of beans? As often as you make this dish, my friend! This is delicious enough to serve to guests, yet simple enough for a casual meal alongside a salad and some bread or rice. Yummmmm…

1½ cups dry adzuki beans
3-inch piece of kombu
2 cups water
½ cup diced onion
2½ teaspoons cumin powder
14.5 oz. can diced tomatoes
14 oz. can coconut milk
¼ cup plus 1 teaspoon fresh lemon juice
2 tablespoons creamy peanut butter
4 medium-large cloves garlic, pressed
2½ teaspoons sea salt (or less)

Garnish:
½ cup chopped fresh cilantro

In a pressure cooker (or a large pot with a tight fitting lid), bring the beans, kombu, water, onion, cumin, tomatoes, and coconut milk to a boil over medium-high heat.
Reduce the heat to low and simmer, covered, until the beans are tender. In a pressure cooker, this will take about 25-35 minutes. In a regular pot, this will usually take about two hours. Am I selling anyone on the idea of a pressure cooker here? Any pressure cooker executives want to give me some money? Once the beans are tender, remove the kombu and stir in the remaining items (all but the cilantro). Serve plain or garnished with cilantro. Yummmm……

Serves 4-6/GF/SF/Blue

Smoky One Pot Beans and Rice

Never thought you could become hopelessly addicted to a bean and rice dish? Think again.

  1 cup long grain brown rice
  2 cups water
  ¼ cup "Chicky Baby Seasoning" (p. 16)
  1 cup lightly packed kale, de-stemmed and cut into thin ribbons
  15 oz. can black or red beans, rinsed and drained
  2 tablespoons extra-virgin olive oil
  4 large cloves garlic, pressed or minced
  1 teaspoon liquid smoke
  ½ teaspoon sea salt

In a pressure cooker or pot with a tight fitting lid, place the rice, water, and "Chicky Baby Seasoning." Bring to a boil over high heat, then simmer over low heat until the rice is tender and the water is fully absorbed. In a pressure cooker, this will take about 20 minutes. In a regular pot, it will take about 45 minutes.

Once the rice is done, stir in the kale immediately so that it wilts from the heat. Add all of the remaining ingredients, stir well, and feel loved—because you are! Leftovers will store, refrigerated in an airtight container, for about a week.

Serves 4/GF/SF/Green

Lemony Lentils with Spinach

This hearty, lowfat dish couldn't be simpler! It's best served over rice or quinoa for a simple, nourishing meal. It's extremely high in fiber, B vitamins, iron, vitamin C, and protein. Dig in and feel great!

  2 cups brown lentils
  6 cups water
  4 cups spinach, washed well
  ½ cup fresh lemon juice
  ¼ cup nutritional yeast
  1 tablespoon extra-virgin olive oil
  1 teaspoon sea salt
  4 large cloves garlic, minced or pressed

Place the lentils and water in a large pot with a tight fitting lid (or a pressure cooker). Bring to a boil over high heat. Reduce heat to low and simmer, covered, until the lentils are completely tender and most of the water has been absorbed. In a pressure cooker, this will take about 20 minutes and in a regular pot, about an hour.

When the lentils are done, remove them from heat and stir in the spinach. Cover for a minute, or until the spinach is wilted. Stir in the remaining ingredients and serve hot over brown rice or quinoa.

Serves 4-6/GF/SF/Green

	Calories Total	Saturated fat (g)	Poly unsat fat (g)	Mono unsat fat (g)	Cholesterol (mg)	Sodium (mg)	Potassium (mg)	Carbohydrate (g)	Dietary fiber (g)	Sugars (g)	Protein (g)
CAB	302	12.4	0	0.2	0	1434	479	27.4	6.8	4.9	8.5
SOPBR	413	1.4	1.6	5.6	0	950	708	67	13	0.7	17.4
LLS	334	0.5	0.7	2.2	0	483	1038	52	25.7	2.3	24.3

Classic Mixed Bean Salad

This fat-free "salad" is perfect as a main dish for summer potlucks, light dinners, and can even be served over spinach or greens.

> One 15 oz. can garbanzo beans (chickpeas)
> One 15 oz. can mixed beans (a blend of kidney beans, pinto beans, and black beans)
> 1 cup thawed, shelled edamame
> ¾ cup minced scallions (green onions)
> ¼ cup apple cider vinegar
> 2 tablespoons EACH: agave nectar and fresh lime juice
> 1 teaspoon ground (dried) yellow mustard powder
> ¾ teaspoon sea salt (or less if you prefer)

Place the garbanzo beans, mixed beans, and edamame in a strainer (over a sink) and rinse well with water. Let drain while you're tossing the remaining items together.

Place all of the remaining ingredients in a medium-large bowl and stir well to combine.

Add the drained beans and edamame to the bowl and gently toss well so that all of the ingredients are thoroughly combined. Voila! Bean happiness at your fingertips. This dish will stay fresh for up to a week when refrigerated in an airtight container.

Serves 4/GF/SF/Green

Bean and Rice Coconut Banana Curry

Although these ingredients might sound a bit odd, I promise you'll love the results. Sweet, spicy, savory, and satisfying—yes, alliteration is necessary under extreme cases of deliciousness.

> 3 cups cooked brown rice
> 1 cup kidney or black beans
> ¼ cup coconut oil
> One banana, sliced (use a banana that is firm and just ripe, not overripe)
> 4 teaspoons fresh lime juice
> 4 medium-large garlic cloves
> 2 teaspoons red curry paste
> ½ teaspoon sea salt
> ½ cup fresh cilantro, chopped

1. Combine the rice, beans, and coconut oil in a pan over low heat, stirring, just until the mixture is thoroughly warmed.

2. Stir in the remaining ingredients (all but the cilantro) until well combined.

3. Garnish with the cilantro and serve.

Serves 3–4/GF/SF/Blue

	Calories	Saturated fat (g)	Poly unsat fat (g)	Mono unsat fat (g)	Cholesterol (mg)	Sodium (mg)	Potassium (mg)	Carbohydrate (g)	Dietary fiber (g)	Sugars (g)	Protein (g)
CMBS	393	0.4	1.5	0.8	0	434	946	68	17.1	15	22.2
BRCBC	563	27.3	1.2	2.4	0	519	490	61	7.3	4.4	8.9

The United Nations reports, "Livestock are responsible for 18% of the greenhouse gases that cause global warming, more than cars, planes and all other forms of transport put together." When the effects of methane (the most potent greenhouse gas emitted from livestocks behinds) is added to the calculation, the estimate of animal foods' contribution to global warming is much higher. Livestock probably contribute to at least 51 percent of total global warming according to World Bank calculations.

Black-eyed Peas with Kale

This simple dish is not only supremely light and nutrient-dense, it's also completely delicious!

- 1½ cups dry black-eyed peas, preferably soaked in water for 8-12 hours
- ½ cup diced onion
- 3 tablespoons "Chicky Baby Seasoning" (p. 16)
- 3½ cups water
- 4 bay leaves
- 4-inch piece of kombu
- 2 cups (packed) kale, preferably lacinato (cut into thin ribbons)
- 6 medium cloves garlic, pressed or minced
- 2 teaspoons EACH: sea salt, nutritional yeast, and olive oil
- ¼ cup fresh lemon juice

To Taste (optional): Hot sauce of your choice (habanero, tabasco, etc.)

Drain the black-eyed peas to remove the soaking water and then rinse them.

Place the beans in a pressure cooker (or regular pot with a tight fitting lid). Add the onion, Chicky Baby, water, bay leaves, and kombu and bring to a boil over high heat. Reduce the heat to low and simmer until the black-eyed peas are tender. This will take about 15 minutes in the pressure cooker (after the top begins to spin) or 45 minutes in a regular pot. If you haven't soaked the peas, it will take about twice as long.

Once them beans is finally done, drain off most of the excess liquid. Remove the bay leaves and kombu. Next, mix in the kale and garlic. Cook over medium-high heat for about 5 minutes, stirring often, until the kale is wilted.

Stir in the salt, nutritional yeast, olive oil, and lemon juice. Top with some of the hot sauce (if using) and serve.

Serves 4/GF/SF/Green

Calories	Saturated fat (g)	Poly unsat fat (g)	Mono unsat fat (g)	Cholesterol (mg)	Sodium (mg)	Potassium (mg)	Carbohydrate (g)	Dietary fiber (g)	Sugars (g)	Protein (g)
294	0.6	0.7	1.8	0	1664	1090	49	9.8	5.8	20

Triathlon Tostadas

This dish may seem complicated, but it can be prepared in under 30 minutes. Plus, any leftovers can easily be stored, so you'll be noshing in style for days! As the name implies, this dish is perfect for endurance, strength, and fitness. They're high in fiber, Omega-3s, vitamins, nutrients, protein, and deliciousness.

Un-fried Tostadas:
6 round corn tortillas, preferably made from sprouted or blue corn
½ tablespoon (1½ teaspoons) oil (olive or melted coconut)

Quinoa Layer:
⅓ cup dry quinoa, rinsed and drained
⅔ cup water
¼ teaspoon sea salt

Black Bean Layer:
15 oz. can black beans (1¾ cups cooked beans), drained and rinsed
1½ tablespoons fresh lime juice
½ teaspoon EACH: cumin powder, onion granules (granulated onion), and sea salt
3 large cloves garlic, minced or pressed
⅛ teaspoon ground cayenne powder

Vivacious Veggies:
½ cup EACH: grated carrots and grated (or chopped) cabbage
3 scallions (green onions), trimmed and finely chopped
1 tablespoon fresh lime juice
1½ avocados, peeled and chopped (¼ avocado per tostada)

1. Preheat your oven to 375° F. Brush or spray the tortillas lightly on both sides with the oil. Next, lay them out on a cookie sheet in a single layer. Bake for 3-5 minutes, then remove from the oven. Flip each tortilla over and place back in the oven for another 3-5 minutes or so (until they are crisp and lightly browned). Be careful not to burn!

2. While your corntillas are transforming into tostada shells, you can perform some other magic. Place the quinoa and water in a small pot with a tight fitting lid. Bring to a boil over medium-high heat. Reduce the heat to low and simmer until all of the water is absorbed, about 15 minutes. Once done, stir in the ¼ teaspoon of sea salt and set aside.

3. To make the black bean mixture, combine all of the items for the black bean layer in a blender or food processor. Blend well until very smooth. Transfer to a small pan and heat over a low flame until warm, stirring occasionally.

4. In a bowl, combine the carrots, cabbage, and scallions with the lime juice. Set aside.

5. Finally, the finish line! To assemble your healthy masterpieces, place the tostada shells on plates and spread with some of the black bean mixture. Sprinkle quinoa over them and add the veggies. Finally, garnish with avocado chunks. You did it! Grab a towel (and don't forget your medal).

Makes 6 tostadas (serves 3-6)/GF/SF/Green

Calories	Saturated fat (g)	Poly unsat fat (g)	Mono unsat fat (g)	Cholesterol (mg)	Sodium (mg)	Potassium (mg)	Carbohydrate (g)	Dietary fiber (g)	Sugars (g)	Protein (g)
362	3.1	2.3	7.1	0	404	865	51	16	2	13.4

Savory Lentils with Caramelized Onions

These high-fiber, low-fat lentils will leave you feeling satisfied, slim, and happy!

Savory Lentils:
1 cup brown lentils
3 cups water
3 tablespoons Chicky Baby Seasoning (p. 16)
3 large cloves garlic, minced or pressed
1 teaspoon balsamic vinegar

Caramelized Onions:
4 cups thinly sliced onion (white or yellow)
1 tablespoon extra-virgin olive oil

For the lentils: Place the lentils, water, and Chicky Baby Seasoning in a pressure cooker or large pot. Bring to a boil over high heat. Simmer until the lentils are tender and most of the water is absorbed. In a pressure cooker, this will take about 25 minutes. In a regular pot, about 45 minutes to an hour.

While the lentils are cooking, set a large skillet over medium-low heat. Add the onions and olive oil. Cook the onions down until they're very well browned and caramelized. This will require stirring the onions every 5-10 minutes or so and adding more water as needed. You'll need to cook the onions for a total of about 45 minutes, so be patient. Your caramelized day will come!

When the lentils are done, stir in the garlic and balsamic vinegar. Serve topped with the delicious caramelized onions.

Serves 4/GF/SF/Green

33

Calories	Saturated fat (g)	Poly unsat fat (g)	Mono unsat fat (g)	Cholesterol (mg)	Sodium (mg)	Potassium (mg)	Carbohydrate (g)	Dietary fiber (g)	Sugars (g)	Protein (g)
272	0.6	0.7	2.6	0	502	743	43	18	6.3	17

Baked Chimichanga

For those of us who used to eat the traditional (deep fried and completely unhealthy) version of these, this recipe is a revelation! Even though my version is low in fat, you'll still end up with a delicious, crispy crust and satisfying flavor. This recipe is for one person, but can easily be multiplied to make more servings.

1 sprouted or whole grain tortilla (or gluten-free tortilla)
½ cup fat-free vegetarian refried beans

Optional Filling Additions:
One whole green chili, roasted and peeled
¼ cup cooked brown rice
2 tablespoons grated vegan cheese (such as Daiya)

Frying Fake-Out:
1 teaspoon oil (preferably coconut or olive)

Fresh Toppings:
½ cup shredded lettuce
Plenty of your favorite organic fresh salsa (or "Francesca's Salsa")
¼ cup minced red or green onions

1. Preheat your oven to 400° F. Lay the tortilla out on a flat surface and place the beans (and any of the optional filling ingredients, if using) in the middle. Fold the sides in, then roll up and over the filling (from the bottom) so that your creation resembles, yes, an enclosed burrito.

2. Place the wrap on an oven-proof pan or cookie sheet. Lightly brush (or spray) the entire wrap with the teaspoon of oil. Place in the oven for 5-10 minutes, or until the bottom has become lightly browned. Turn over and bake another 5-10 minutes, or until the entire tortilla is nicely browned and crisp. Remove from the oven.

3. Place the chimichanga on a plate and top with lettuce, salsa, and onions. Enjoy!

Serves 1/GF/SF/Green

Calories	Saturated fat (g)	Poly unsat fat (g)	Mono unsat fat (g)	Cholesterol (mg)	Sodium (mg)	Potassium (mg)	Carbohydrate (g)	Dietary fiber (g)	Sugars (g)	Protein (g)
593	6.2	0.9	0.7	0	1484	893	100	12.7	7.8	22.6

Summery Chickpea Toss

This flavorful dish is the perfect answer to a hot summer day! Serve along with some whole grain bread and vegetable soup for a hearty, yet light meal.

Two 15 oz. cans chickpeas (garbanzo beans), drained and rinsed
2 cups thinly sliced cucumber
1 cup chopped tomato
½ cup EACH: chopped fresh basil and chopped fresh parsley
¼ cup fresh lemon juice
1 tablespoon extra-virgin olive oil
4 large cloves garlic, minced or pressed
1 teaspoon sea salt
½ teaspoon black pepper

In a medium-large bowl, combine all of the ingredients. Stir well. Serve cold or at room temperature.

Serves 4/GF/SF/Green

Ful Mudhamas

I first tried this dish at a wonderful Mid-Eastern restaurant. Although they used fava beans for authenticity, I've found that pinto beans can fill almost anyone.

3 cups (or two 15 oz. cans) cooked and drained fava or pinto beans (unsalted)
4 teaspoons extra-virgin (or regular) olive oil
3 tablespoons plus 1 teaspoon fresh lemon juice
2 tablespoons (packed) minced fresh cilantro or parsley
¾ teaspoon sea salt (or less if you prefer)
2 small-medium cloves garlic, minced or pressed

Toss everything together and mix well. Serve at room temperature or cold. This will store refrigerated in an airtight container for several days.

Serves 4/GF/SF/Green

	Calories	Saturated fat (g)	Poly unsat fat (g)	Mono unsat fat (g)	Cholesterol (mg)	Sodium (mg)	Potassium (mg)	Carbohydrate (g)	Dietary fiber (g)	Sugars (g)	Protein (g)
SCT	407	1.1	2.9	3.8	0	583	898	64	17.6	12.7	20.3
FM	279	0.8	0.9	3.5	0	431	594	43.4	11.6	4.2	16.3

Black Bean and Rice Bowl with Mango Salsa

So yeah, I could eat this every day. I love how the abundance of flavorful, fresh salsa brings all the other ingredients to life!

Mango Salsa:
2 cups diced mango (the flesh of about 2 large mangoes)
¼ cup EACH: finely minced white onion and chopped cilantro
2 tablespoons fresh lime juice
¼ teaspoon EACH: sea salt and dried chili (red pepper) flakes

Salad:
2 cups cooked brown rice
1½ cups cooked black beans (one can of black beans, drained and rinsed)
3/4 cup EACH: grated carrots and chopped or grated red cabbage

Make the mango salsa: Toss all of the salsa ingredients together in a medium bowl until well combined and overly enticing. Set aside.

Layer the salad ingredients in a bowl. Top with the salsa and serve. Enjoy your colorful, health-promoting fiesta in a bowl!

Serves 2/GF/SF/Green

Calories	Saturated fat (g)	Poly unsat fat (g)	Mono unsat fat (g)	Cholesterol (mg)	Sodium (mg)	Potassium (mg)	Carbohydrate (g)	Dietary fiber (g)	Sugars (g)	Protein (g)
532	0.7	1	0.8	0	322	1108	113	20	28.4	17.9

Francesca's Salsa

What would Mexican bean dishes be without a great salsa? Not much, my friends. When I first met my mother-in-law Francesca, she kept a constant supply of this freshly made salsa for us, along with refried Peruvian beans and fresh guacamole. It was one of the most satisfying food experiences of my life. Thank you, Francesca!

> 28 oz. can diced tomatoes
> ½ cup finely chopped onion (white or yellow)
> ½ cup finely chopped green onion (both white and green parts)
> ¼ cup minced jalapeno
> ¼ cup chopped cilantro
> 8 large cloves garlic, minced or pressed
> 1½ teaspoons sea salt

Optional: 2 chiles de arbol (dried or fresh)

In a food processor or blender, add the can of tomatoes, including all of the liquid. Blend briefly until fairly smooth, but leave in a bit of texture.

Remove to a bowl or airtight container and stir in the remaining ingredients. If you like lots of heat (great for your metabolism!), add the chiles de arbol as well. If they're fresh, mince them—if they're dried, crumble them into the salsa.

This is best when the flavors are allowed to marry overnight. Serve cold with baked tortilla chips, bean burritos, tostadas, or any other delicious plant-based bean dish you can dream up!

Francesca says: "If something seems like it's missing from your salsa, it's probably garlic. Add lots and lots of garlic!"

Makes about 5 cups of salsa/GF/SF/Green

	Calories	Saturated fat (g)	Poly unsat fat (g)	Mono unsat fat (g)	Cholesterol (mg)	Sodium (mg)	Potassium (mg)	Carbohydrate (g)	Dietary fiber (g)	Sugars (g)	Protein (g)
FS	94	0.2	0.1	0	0	1432	157	17.8	2.7	10.7	4.4
TSCLS	440	1.4	3.3	3.3	0	1019	1240	72	17.8	12.7	23.8

Taco Salad with Chipotle Lime Sauce

What possible excuse could you make for not trying this? I don't even want to hear it. Make this immediately.

Chipotle Lime Sauce:
12.3 oz package of silken tofu (firm), drained (water poured off)
¼ cup plus 1 tablespoon fresh lime juice
4 teaspoons (packed) brown sugar
3 large cloves garlic, peeled
1 teaspoon lime zest (the zest of one large lime)
1 teaspoon sea salt
½ teaspoon ground chipotle powder

Baked Chipotle Chips:
8 corn tortillas
2 teaspoons olive oil (or olive oil spray)
¼ teaspoon EACH: sea salt and ground chipotle powder

Salad:
6 cups romaine lettuce, chopped
1 cup EACH: chopped tomato and chopped cabbage
2 cups cooked black beans, seasoned with salt if desired
½ cup chopped cilantro
¼ cup diced onion

Place all of the ingredients for the Chipotle Lime Sauce in a blender. Blend until totally smooth and emulsified. Set aside.

Preheat your oven to 400 F. Spray a large baking sheet with oil (or brush lightly with oil). Cut the tortillas into quarters, making a total of 32 tortilla chips. Spray or lightly brush the chips with oil and sprinkle evenly with the salt and chipotle powder. Bake for 5-10 minutes, or until crisp and lightly browned. Set aside.

In large bowls, place the lettuce, tomato, cabbage, beans, cilantro, and onion. Surround with the chips and drizzle with the Chipotle Lime Sauce. Serve immediately.

Serves 2-4/ GF/Green

Moroccan French Lentils

Yeah, I might be really bad at geography, but don't blame the lentils. This dish is a yummy one-pot wonder, perfect for eating light and healthy on the run!

1 cup French lentils
½ cup EACH: orange juice and
   pomegranate juice
2½ cups water
4 whole cloves
1½ teaspoons EACH: ground cumin and
   ground cinnamon
2 tablespoons agave nectar
Optional: Pinch of saffron

Last Additions:
1 cup kale ribbons (washed and de-stemmed
   kale, chopped)
¾ teaspoon sea salt

Place all of the ingredients (except for the last additions) in a pressure cooker or large pot with a tight fitting lid. Stir well and bring to a boil over high heat. Reduce heat to low and simmer until the lentils are tender (although French lentils will still be somewhat firm). This will take about 25 minutes in a pressure cooker or 45 minutes in a regular pot. Remove from heat and stir in the last additions. Cover immediately and allow to sit until the kale has wilted and become edibly tender, about 5 minutes. Enjoy!

Serves 4-6/GF/SF/Green

Calories	Saturated fat (g)	Poly unsat fat (g)	Mono unsat fat (g)	Cholesterol (mg)	Sodium (mg)	Potassium (mg)	Carbohydrate (g)	Dietary fiber (g)	Sugars (g)	Protein (g)
196	0.1	0.3	0.2	0	352	549	37.7	12.6	12.4	10.7

Rosemary White Beans with Artichokes

Here's an example of how a simple bean dish can become elevated to an impressive entrée just by using a few gourmet ingredients that pack lots of flavor!

Where Have You Bean All My Life?
1 cup dry great white northern beans, soaked in plenty of water for 8-12 hours
2 teaspoons dried rosemary leaf
2-inch piece of kombu
2 bay leaves
2½ cups water
2 tablespoons "Chicky Baby Seasoning" (p. 16)

Stir It Up:
½ teaspoon sea salt
1 tablespoon extra-virgin olive oil
2 teaspoons fresh lemon juice
3 medium-large cloves garlic, minced or pressed
¾ cup marinated artichoke hearts, drained

Fresh Finale:
1 tablespoon (packed) fresh basil, sliced thinly into ribbons
2 tablespoons julienne sliced, marinated sun-dried tomatoes

Drain and rinse the beans. Place in a large, covered pot (or pressure cooker) with the dried rosemary, kombu, bay leaves, water, and Chicky Baby. Bring to a boil, then reduce the heat to low and simmer until the beans are tender. In a pressure cooker, this will take about 25-35 minutes. In a regular pot, this will usually take 1-2 hours.

When the beans are tender, drain off any excess liquid and remove the kombu and bay leaves. Stir in the salt, oil, lemon juice, garlic, and artichokes.

Serve topped with the basil and tomatoes.

Serves 4/GF/SF/Green

Calories	Saturated fat (g)	Poly unsat fat (g)	Mono unsat fat (g)	Cholesterol (mg)	Sodium (mg)	Potassium (mg)	Carbohydrate (g)	Dietary fiber (g)	Sugars (g)	Protein (g)
232	0.8	0.7	2.9	0	712	823	33.1	10.9	1.3	12.9

8 Minute Enchiladas

Fast, delicious, and satisfying – all while supporting your healthy weight goals? YES please!

- 2 corn tortillas
- ½ cup cooked beans (pinto or black beans work well)
- 1/3 cup vegan enchilada sauce ("Simply Organic" makes a nice dry enchilada sauce mix)
- 2 tablespoons shredded vegan cheddar cheese (such as "Daiya")

Topping:
- 3 tablespoons EACH: minced onion and chopped fresh cilantro

Heat a medium skillet over low heat. Place the corn tortillas in the skillet and cover them with a lid until they're warm. Letting them warm up will keep them from breaking apart when you roll them.

Place the beans along the center of each tortilla. Roll up and place seam-side down in the pan. Cover and cook for 3 minutes over medium-high heat.

While they're cooking, prepare the topping items and heat up the enchilada sauce until very hot.

Flip the enchiladas over and cook for another 3 minutes, covered. Remove the enchiladas to a plate, top with hot enchilada sauce, and sprinkle with cheese. Add the onion and cilantro and serve. Yum!

Serves 1/GF/SF/Green

	Calories	Saturated fat (g)	Poly unsat fat (g)	Mono unsat fat (g)	Cholesterol (mg)	Sodium (mg)	Potassium (mg)	Carbohydrate (g)	Dietary fiber (g)	Sugars (g)	Protein (g)
8ME	286	1.3	0.7	0.3	0	838	435	50.4	12.3	7	12
SQQ	582	3.2	.3	0.1	0	719	611	98	14.1	2.8	24

Spinach Quinoa Quesadillas

This incredibly quick dish always reminds me of my dear clients and friends, the Weilers. I taught them how to rock a healthy plant-based diet back in 2012 (and they've been thriving since). This has been their favorite go-to dish as it's easy to make, filling, and yummy. They've gotten so good at making it, in fact, that their quesadillas are now better than mine!

One whole grain tortilla
½ cup cooked black beans
¼ cup EACH: minced onion, cooked quinoa, and vegan cheese (such as Daiya)
1 cup (lightly packed) fresh baby spinach
Optional: Francesca's Salsa (or salsa of your choice)

1. Prepare all of the ingredients you'll be using and set them aside.

2. Set a large skillet over medium heat. Place the tortilla on the skillet and evenly distribute the beans, onion, quinoa, vegan cheese, and spinach over half of the tortilla. Fold the other half of the tortilla over and cover the quesadilla with a lid or press. Cook for about 4 minutes.

3. Gently flip the quesadilla over and cook the other side for 4 minutes, or until both sides are golden-browned and crisp. Remove from heat, cut in half, and serve. If desired, top with some salsa.

Serves 1/SF/Green

Tip: For this dish (or any other simple, healthy favorite), you can make your life easier by doing the prepwork in advance. For example, you can keep cooked beans and quinoa in the fridge, along with your favorite salsa. That makes preparation time for this dish a mere one minute!

Mung Beans with Cilantro Chutney

This yummy, homey dish is very low in calories yet high in fiber—so it will fill you up without filling you out!

Mung Beans:
1½ cups mung beans
4 cups water
1 tablespoon cumin seeds
3 tablespoons fresh lime juice
1 teaspoon ground coriander
1 teaspoon sea salt

Cilantro Chutney:
½ cup (packed) fresh cilantro
1½ tablespoons finely shredded coconut
1 tablespoon EACH: chopped fresh ginger and dry-roasted peanuts
2 small-medium cloves garlic, peeled
½ small jalapeno, seeded (or less if you prefer your chutney less spicy)
½ teaspoon cumin seeds
¼ teaspoon sea salt
1 tablespoon fresh lime juice
¼ cup water

1. First, begin the mung beans: Place the mung beans, water, and cumin seeds in a large pot or pressure cooker. Bring to a boil over high heat, then reduce heat to low. Simmer until the beans are tender and the water is absorbed—this will take about 20 minutes in a pressure cooker or 40 minutes in a regular pot.

2. While the beans are cooking, make the chutney: In a food processor or blender, place all of the chutney ingredients. Blend well until the mixture is thoroughly combined – you will want to retain a little texture, but not too much!

3. When the beans are done, stir in the lime juice, coriander, and sea salt thoroughly. Serve the beans in bowls, topped with the cilantro chutney.

Serves 4/GF/SF/Green

Calories	Saturated fat (g)	Poly unsat fat (g)	Mono unsat fat (g)	Cholesterol (mg)	Sodium (mg)	Potassium (mg)	Carbohydrate (g)	Dietary fiber (g)	Sugars (g)	Protein (g)
115	0.8	0.5	0.9	0	714	308	18.4	6.5	2.2	6.5

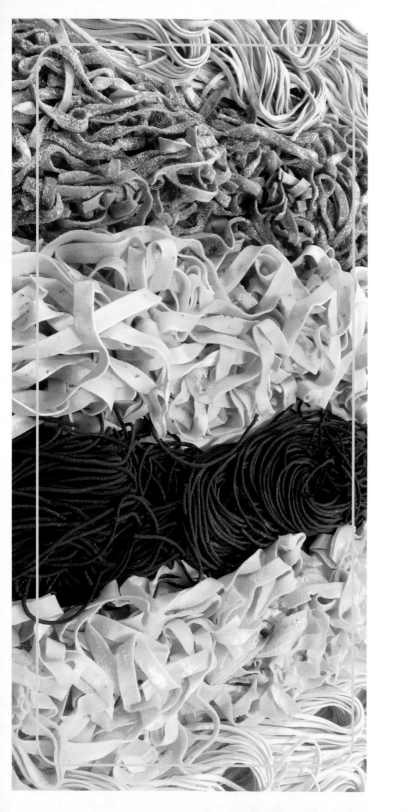
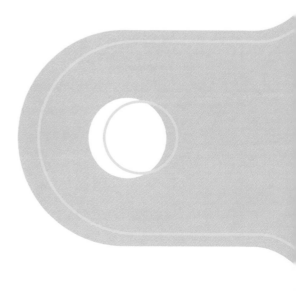

Power Pasta

Pasta as a weight loss food? Yup, you're not dreaming—you can actually eat pasta and thrive! These days, there is a wide variety of whole grain pasta varieties on the market, so you can thoroughly enjoy this comfort food without the heavy-tasting whole grain pastas of yore. Plus, pasta is the perfect vehicle for all sorts of vitalizing superfoods. So power up and enjoy!

Perfect Pasta

Why perfect? Well, this dish perfectly satisfies that craving for Italian pasta that so many of us have (and unfortunately feel guilty about!), but in a whole-grain, healthy way. Indulge and enjoy!

8 oz. whole grain linguine

Sauce:
1 tablespoon EACH: extra-virgin olive oil and balsamic vinegar
15 oz. can crushed tomatoes, lightly drained
4–5 medium cloves garlic, pressed or minced
2 teaspoons dried oregano
¼ cup (packed) fresh basil, cut into thin ribbons
1 teaspoon sea salt
Freshly ground pepper to taste

1. Begin cooking the linguine according to the directions on the package.

2. While the noodles are cooking, place the ingredients for the sauce in a large bowl. When the linguine is al dente, drain well and toss with the sauce. Serve immediately. Enjoy!

Serves 4/GF (with substitution)/SF/Green

Chickpea Artichoke Pasta Toss

Picnic, anyone? This delicious dish always reminds me of summer—even though I sometimes cheat and eat it mid-winter! The abundance of vegetables (and the addition of beans) makes this even more light and healthy, so dig in and feel fantastic!

8 oz. corn-quinoa pasta shells or twists
15 oz. can chickpeas, rinsed and drained
15 oz. can quartered artichoke hearts, drained
1 cup EACH: chopped cucumber and grape (or cherry) tomatoes
½ cup EACH: diced onion (white or yellow) and chopped kalamata olives
¼ cup (packed) fresh basil, cut into ribbons
3 tablespoons fresh lemon juice
2 tablespoons extra-virgin olive oil
4-5 large cloves garlic, minced or pressed
1 teaspoon EACH: sea salt and black pepper
4 cups spinach

Cook the pasta until al dente, according to the directions on the package. Drain well and set aside.

Toss the remaining ingredients (all but the baby greens) in a large bowl. Add the pasta and stir gently to combine. Serve over the spinach and enjoy!

Serves 4-6/GF/SF/Green

49

	Calories	Saturated fat (g)	Poly unsat fat (g)	Mono unsat fat (g)	Cholesterol (mg)	Sodium (mg)	Potassium (mg)	Carbohydrate (g)	Dietary fiber (g)	Sugars (g)	Protein (g)
PP	282	0.6	0.5	2.6	0	706	346	57	6.4	0.7	6.2
CAPT	419	1.2	1.7	4.5	0	852	545	71	14.4	6.9	13.8

Ten Minute Pasta with Artichokes

Why? Because artichokes.

    8 oz. dry corn-quinoa pasta (I use "Ancient Harvest" brand)
    Two 15 oz. cans or jars of water-packed artichoke hearts, drained and quartered
    3 tablespoons extra-virgin olive oil
    8 cloves garlic, pressed or minced
    ¼ cup fresh parsley, minced
    Lots of freshly ground black pepper to taste
    Sea salt to taste (try truffle salt for extra deliciousness)

Cook the pasta according to the directions on the package.

While the pasta is cooking, place all of the other ingredients in a large bowl and toss well.

Once the pasta is al dente, drain and toss with the "sauce." Serve immediately.

Serves 4/GF/SF/Blue

Stacey's Cheesy Kelp Noodles

Confession: I used to despise kelp noodles. I couldn't understand what so many people saw in them. Sure, I knew how nutritious they were—super high in calcium, iodine, and minerals, yet almost calorie-free. But still, that unusually crunchy texture just threw me off. Then, one day I tried a bite of Stacey's cheesy kelp noodles. (Stacey is our amazing assistant and also my soul sister and cousin.) She had combined a bag of kelp noodles with some of my cheesy sauce mix and what resulted was a bowl of perfection. Thank you, Stacey!

    1/3 cup "Cheesy Mix" (p. 99)
    2/3 cup water
    12 oz. bag kelp noodles, rinsed

Place the Cheesy Mix in a small pot along with the water and stir. Bring to a boil over medium-high heat, whisking well. Reduce heat to low and continue to whisk until the mixture has thickened. Remove from heat.

Stir the cheesy sauce into the noodles and toss well. The ultimate nutrient-dense, low-calorie indulgence awaits!

Serves 1-2/GF/SF/Green

Garlic Veggie Noodle Bowl, Your Way

Introducing the perfect guilt-free pasta fix! It's easy, yummy, and quick, especially if you have cooked noodles and pre-cut veggies on hand. You'll notice that I've given a range of amounts for the garlic and chili sauce. Personally, I always use the high end of that range for maximum flavor. However, this is your noodle bowl (hence, the title). Have fun experimenting and making it just right for you!

> 1 cup cooked whole grain noodles (your choice), about 2 oz. dry
> 1 teaspoon toasted sesame oil
> 1 tablespoon tamari, divided
> 1–3 medium cloves peeled garlic, cut into thin slices
> 2 cups veggies, your choice (You can use just one kind or mix and match)
> 1–3 cloves garlic, minced or pressed
> 1–3 teaspoons spicy chili sauce
> 1 teaspoon toasted sesame seeds

If you haven't cooked your noodles yet, do so now. When they're al dente, drain them well and set aside.

In a large skillet or wok set to medium-high heat, add the oil, half of the tamari, the sliced garlic, and your veggies. However, if you're using all quick cooking veggies (such as bok choy and peapods), you'll want to brown the garlic first before adding the veggies.

Stir-fry the veggie-garlic mixture, stirring often, until the garlic is browned and your veggies are crisp-tender.

Gently stir in the noodles, remaining garlic and tamari, and chili sauce until well combined. Serve in a bowl, topped with the sesame seeds. Now it's time to get your noodle fix—and feel good about it!

> Serves 1/GF (if using gluten-free noodles)/Green

	Calories	Saturated fat (g)	Poly unsat fat (g)	Mono unsat fat (g)	Cholesterol (mg)	Sodium (mg)	Potassium (mg)	Carbohydrate (g)	Dietary fiber (g)	Sugars (g)	Protein (g)
TMPA	365	1.5	1.2	7.5	0	756	46.8	59	10.9	1.7	7.8
SCKN	236	1.3	1.4	3.9	0	1366	626	24.8	9.4	1.2	17
GVNB	545	1	2.8	2.4	0	1355	715	103	20.8	15.4	17.6

Orange Ginger Veggie Noodle Bowl

I would be flat-out lying to you if I said I wasn't craving a big bowl of these right this minute. Serious deliciousness is happening here, people. But not only that—the crunchy vegetables and superfood ingredients make this a supremely vitalizing dish as well. You can thank me later. . . with a bowl of these noodles.

8 oz. whole grain rice noodles, the kind you would use for Pad Thai (I use Annie Chun's brown rice noodles)

Veggies:
2 cups broccoli, chopped into bite-sized pieces
1 cup diced or thinly sliced zucchini
1 cup julienne-cut (or diced) carrot

Orange Ginger Sauce:
½ cup fresh orange juice (about the juice of one large orange)
2 teaspoons minced orange zest (about the zest of one large orange)
3 tablespoons EACH: tamari and agave nectar
1 tablespoon oil (sunflower or non-virgin olive)
2 tablespoons grated fresh ginger
4 large cloves garlic, minced or pressed
¼ – ½ teaspoon red chili flakes (I use ½ teaspoon, but I like my food spicy!)

Prepare the noodles according to the directions on their package.

While the noodles are cooking, you can get the rest of the dish ready. To begin, place the broccoli in a medium pan with a little water. Stir-fry for about 2 minutes, then add the zucchini. Stir-fry (adding more water if needed) for another 2 minutes, or until they are both bright green and crisp-tender. Stir in the carrots, remove from heat, and set aside.

Place all of the ingredients for the Orange Ginger Sauce in a large bowl. Stir well and set aside.

When the pasta is al dente, drain well and add to the large bowl along with the vegetables. Gently stir well to combine and serve.

Serves 4/GF/Blue

Calories	Saturated fat (g)	Poly unsat fat (g)	Mono unsat fat (g)	Cholesterol (mg)	Sodium (mg)	Potassium (mg)	Carbohydrate (g)	Dietary fiber (g)	Sugars (g)	Protein (g)
358	1	1.2	2	0	813	690	72	7.8	21.3	9.1

Drunken Noodles

This is a lower-fat, quicker version of my "Thai Drunken Noodles" from Radiant Health, Inner Wealth. It still contains all the potent nutrients, antioxidants, and immune-boosting ingredients, as well as a delicious punch of flavor! Consider these Drunken Noodles as the perfect way to *Get Waisted*.

> 8 oz. whole grain rice noodles, the kind you would use for Pad Thai (I use Annie Chun's brown rice noodles)
>
> 1 cup (packed) cilantro, washed well and chopped
> ½ cup green onions, chopped
> ¼ cup EACH: tamari and fresh lime juice
> 2 tablespoons grated ginger
> 4 large cloves garlic, minced or pressed
> 1 tablespoon agave nectar
> 2 teaspoons toasted sesame oil
> 1 teaspoon ground turmeric
> ¼ teaspoon ground cayenne

1. Cook the noodles al dente according to the directions on their package.

2. You can assemble the rest of this dish while the noodles are cooking—Simply place the remaining ingredients in a large bowl. Stir well and set aside until the noodles are done.

3. Once the noodles are al dente, drain them well and toss them with the sauce and vegetables in the bowl. Stir them gently yet thoroughly. Serve immediately.

Serves 2-4/GF/Green

If you're turning over the box of food to look at the nutrition label, chances are, you are making a poor choice. Real, whole foods don't have labels. Spend your time choosing healthier whole foods, instead of learning to read labels. It will get you to your health goals much more quickly!

	Calories	Saturated fat (g)	Poly unsat fat (g)	Mono unsat fat (g)	Cholesterol (mg)	Sodium (mg)	Potassium (mg)	Carbohydrate (g)	Dietary fiber (g)	Sugars (g)	Protein (g)
DN	353	1.2	1.3	1.2	0	1360	175	71	6.4	8.2	8.6
CLNR	372	1.4	1.9	3.2	0	798	182	69	6.7	5	8.9

Chili Lime Noodles to the Rescue

This is my go-to dish for a million reasons—the main one being the deliciousness factor. But also, with the abundance of vitalizing superfoods in this dish, it's pretty much the feel-good noodle party of the year!

8 oz. whole grain rice noodles, the kind you would use for Pad Thai (I use Annie Chun's brown rice noodles)
¼ cup fresh lime juice
¼ cup grated fresh ginger
2 tablespoons tamari
1 tablespoon sriracha sauce (or more if you like heat!)
2 teaspoons oil (sunflower or non-virgin olive)
5 medium-large garlic cloves, minced or pressed
½ cup (packed) fresh cilantro, chopped
4 green onions, trimmed and finely chopped
2 tablespoons dry roasted peanuts, crushed

1. Prepare the noodles according to the directions on their package.

2. While the noodles are cooking, you can get the rest of the dish ready. In a large bowl, place the remaining ingredients (all but the peanuts). Stir well.

3. When the pasta is al dente, drain well and add to the large bowl. Gently stir well to combine. Serve cold or at room temperature, topped with the crushed peanuts.

Serves 2-4/GF/Green

All Better Noodle Bowl

This dish was born when I needed something fast, easy, and immune-boosting while I was fighting a cold. Sure enough, I felt better by the next day! Every single ingredient has superpowers, as far as your health and immunity are concerned. But of course, you're welcome to make this even when you're feeling great and just want something quick, delicious, and comforting!

   One bundle soba noodles
   1 cup sliced shiitake mushrooms
   ¼ cup water
   1 tablespoon red or dark miso
   2 large cloves garlic, minced or pressed
   2 teaspoons ginger, grated

Boil the noodles according to the directions on the package. Be careful not to overcook, as soba noodles cook very quickly. Drain and set aside.

Meanwhile, sauté the mushrooms in the water until they're tender. Transfer to a bowl and add the miso. Whisk the miso with the water until smooth.

Add all of the remaining ingredients to the bowl, including the noodles, and serve. Feel better!

Serves 1/Green

Lo Fat Lo Mein

This tasty dish is chock-full of life-enhancing veggies and will healthfully satisfy that craving for Chinese takeout!

   8.8 oz. whole grain pasta (or soba noodles)
   2 teaspoons toasted (dark) sesame oil
   2 tablespoons liquid vegetarian broth
   Small onion, sliced very thinly
   1 cup diced (or julienne cut) zucchini
   2 cups thinly sliced shiitake mushroom caps
   Medium carrot, julienne cut or diced
   2 cups chopped napa cabbage
   1 tablespoon grated fresh ginger
   5 medium cloves garlic, minced or pressed
   4 tablespoons tamari, shoyu, or soy sauce (or less if you prefer)
   1 tablespoon agave nectar
   ½ teaspoon (or more to taste) dried red chili flakes
   1 teaspoon arrowroot

Garnish:
   1 tablespoon toasted sesame seeds

1. Prepare all of the vegetables (onion, zucchini, shiitakes, carrot, and cabbage) and set them aside individually (do not mix all of the veggies together as they will cook at different rates). If you like, get the ginger and garlic ready for the big show as well.

2. Boil the noodles according to the directions on their package. While the noodles are cooking, skip to step three. When the noodles are al dente, drain them and gently toss with one teaspoon of the toasted sesame oil. Set aside until step six.

	Calories	Saturated fat (g)	Poly unsat fat (g)	Mono unsat fat (g)	Cholesterol (mg)	Sodium (mg)	Potassium (mg)	Carbohydrate (g)	Dietary fiber (g)	Sugars (g)	Protein (g)
ABNB	434	0.4	0.8	0.5	0	1377	477	96	4.2	1.2	17.9
LFLM	363	0.6	1.5	1.4	0	1063	362	75	7.6	6.7	9.5

3. While the noodles are cooking, you should be able to prepare the rest of the dish. Place the other one teaspoon of the toasted sesame oil in a wok (or very large skillet) along with the broth. Sauté the onion for about 5-6 minutes over medium-high heat, until soft and lightly browned.

4. Add the zucchini and shiitakes to the onion mixture and cook until the zucchini becomes softened as well. This should take about 3-5 minutes.

5. Add the carrot, cabbage, ginger, garlic, tamari, agave, and chili flakes to the wok. Lightly sprinkle the arrowroot evenly over the mixture and stir it in immediately to prevent lumping. Continue to sauté over medium heat until the cabbage is wilted and all of the ingredients are well combined, about 2-3 minutes.

6. Add the noodles to the wok and gently toss with the veggies until well combined. If you prefer a saucier situation, you can add just a little more liquid broth to the mixture and stir it in well.

7. Serve topped with the toasted sesame seeds. This will keep for up to one week in the fridge.

Serves 4/GF (with rice noodles)/Green

Vitality Noodles

As the name implies, you may feel like running a marathon after eating this dish! The abundance of fresh ginger and garlic are part of the magic, as they are renowned immune boosters and detoxifying agents. The fresh lime juice and veggies also add to the vitamin party. Because this is so low in fat, it also feels very "clean."

2 "nests" bean thread noodles (about 3½ oz. total)

Vitamin Party:
3 tablespoons fresh lime juice
1 teaspoon toasted (dark) sesame oil
2½ tablespoons tamari, shoyu, or soy sauce
3 medium-large cloves garlic, minced or pressed
1½ tablespoons grated fresh ginger
¼ cup minced cilantro
One scallion (green onion), trimmed and diced (about 2 tablespoons)
One small carrot, julienne cut or diced (about 2 tablespoons)
¼ cup diced cucumber (peeled if non-organic)

Garnish:
2 tablespoons toasted sesame seeds

1. Cook the beanthread noodles according to the directions on their package.

2. While the noodles are soaking, place all of the other ingredients (except for the sesame seeds) in a medium sized bowl.

3. When the noodles are soft, drain them well. Cut the noodles a few times with a sharp knife (or kitchen scissors), as this will help them to mix into the toppings more evenly.

4. Place the noodles into the party that's happening in the medium sized bowl. Combine thoroughly with a large spoon. Serve this dish cold or at room temperature, topped with the toasted sesame seeds. Do not heat this dish at any point, however, as it may ruin the freshness mojo.

Serves 2-4/GF/Green

	Calories	Saturated fat (g)	Poly unsat fat (g)	Mono unsat fat (g)	Cholesterol (mg)	Sodium (mg)	Potassium (mg)	Carbohydrate (g)	Dietary fiber (g)	Sugars (g)	Protein (g)
VN	193	0.7	2	1.7	0	856	187	35.7	1.8	1.8	3.3
PPM	315	0.8	0.6	3.8	0	431	317	60	5.5	2.4	6.8

Pasta Prezzemolo with Mushrooms

This parsley mushroom pasta is perfect for when you need a quick but healthy pasta fix!

8 oz. pasta
2½ cups sliced mushrooms (crimini or portabella)
1 teaspoon plus 1 tablespoon extra-virgin olive oil
2 tablespoons balsamic vinegar, divided
1 teaspoon tamari
6 medium cloves garlic, minced or pressed (divided)
½ cup (packed) minced parsley
1 teaspoon minced rosemary, fresh or dried
½ teaspoon EACH: sea salt and black pepper

Cook the pasta al dente according to the directions on the package. Drain and set aside.

In a large skillet set to medium heat, sauté the mushrooms with 1 teaspoon of the oil, 1 tablespoon of the vinegar, the tamari, and 3 of the garlic cloves. Stir often and cook until the mushrooms are tender and nicely browned, about 5-10 minutes.

Remove from heat and add the remaining ingredients to the skillet. Stir well to combine.

Add the cooked, drained pasta to the skillet and toss gently to thoroughly combine with the remaining ingredients. Serve warm or hot.

Serves 3-4/GF (if using gluten-free pasta)/ Green

Pasta Caulifredo

Imagine a bowl of comforting noodles smothered in loads of creamy white sauce, yet totally guilt free! This dish is high in fiber, veggie-laden, vitamin-rich, and free from oils. Can you even imagine such a thing? Wait, you don't have to—just make this dish and see for yourself!

1 lb. whole grain pasta, any kind
½ cup chopped parsley

Caulifredo Sauce:
One medium head cauliflower (7 cups chopped cauliflower)
2 cups water
½ cup EACH: raw cashews and nutritional yeast
4 large cloves garlic, peeled
1 tablespoon EACH: mellow white miso and umeboshi (ume plum) vinegar
½ teaspoon EACH: sea salt and black pepper

Steam the cauliflower until tender. This will take you about 15 minutes.

While the cauliflower is steaming, cook your pasta according to the package directions. Once al dente, drain and set aside.

For the Caulifredo Sauce: Place the steamed, tender cauliflower in a good blender or food processor (preferably a Vitamix or other high-speed blender). Add the cashews and one cup of the water. Blend, blend, blend until very smooth. Add the remaining sauce ingredients and blend until completely smooth and creamy.

Serve the pasta topped with a generous amount of the sauce. Sprinkle with parsley and serve.

Serves 8/GF (if using gluten-free pasta)/Green

Feel Good Mac 'N Cheese

This creamy macaroni and cheese is totally satisfying, yet devoid of the junk that usually accompanies this comfort food. Plus, the addition of several vitalizing superfoods will leave your soul feeling satisfied and your body feeling nourished!

8 oz. whole grain pasta elbows (I use "Ancient Harvest" corn-quinoa pasta)
¼ cup EACH: nutritional yeast powder and unsweetened nondairy milk
2 tablespoons oil (raw sesame, olive, or melted non-virgin coconut)
½ tablespoon mellow white miso
1-2 medium cloves garlic, minced or pressed
1 teaspoon mustard powder
½ teaspoon sea salt

Optional: 2 tablespoons chopped parsley and/or minced chives

1. Boil the pasta until al dente according to the instructions on the package.

2. Meanwhile, whisk all of the remaining ingredients (aside from the parsley) together until very smooth.

3. Once the pasta is done, drain well and toss with the sauce. Serve immediately. If desired, garnish with the parsley and/or chives.

Serves 2-4/GF/Blue

	Calories	Saturated fat (g)	Poly unsat fat (g)	Mono unsat fat (g)	Cholesterol (mg)	Sodium (mg)	Potassium (mg)	Carbohydrate (g)	Dietary fiber (g)	Sugars (g)	Protein (g)
PC	304	0.6	0.7	1.7	0	648	467	56	8.1	2	11.7
FGMNC	414	7.9	0.3	0.7	0	497	269	67	8.5	0.3	12.7

Thai Red Curry Noodles

These flavorful, saucy noodles boast loads of antioxidants—plus, they come together in under 30 minutes! Perfection happens, and when it does I like to sit back, laugh, and eat red curry noodles.

  8 oz. whole grain rice noodles, the kind you would use for Pad Thai (I use Annie Chun's brown rice noodles)
  2 tablespoons Thai red curry paste (such as Thai Kitchen brand)
  One 14 oz. can lowfat coconut milk
  5 large cloves garlic, minced or pressed
  2 tablespoons grated fresh ginger
  ½ cup (packed) EACH: finely chopped green onions and chopped cilantro
  ¼ cup fresh lime juice
  ¼ cup (packed) fresh basil, cut into thin ribbons
  1 teaspoon sea salt

1. Prepare the noodles according to the directions on their package.

2. While the noodles are cooking, you can get the rest of the dish together. In a large bowl, place the curry paste and a little of the coconut milk. Whisk together until smooth. Add the remaining coconut milk and whisk again until emulsified.

3. Add the remaining ingredients to the bowl and stir well.

4. Once the noodles are al dente, drain them very well and add them to the bowl. Stir gently to thoroughly combine. Serve at room temperature.

  Serves 4/GF/SF/Green

Calories	Saturated fat (g)	Poly unsat fat (g)	Mono unsat fat (g)	Cholesterol (mg)	Sodium (mg)	Potassium (mg)	Carbohydrate (g)	Dietary fiber (g)	Sugars (g)	Protein (g)
299	6.3	0	0	0	1100	78	51	4.5	1.8	4.6

Pasta with Banzoballs

This twist on traditional pasta with meatballs is not only extremely fun to say – it's also delicious, high in fiber, low in fat, and a huge hit with both kids and adults!

1 lb. whole grain pasta
Organic, vegan pasta sauce

Banzoballs:
2 tablespoons EACH: water and tamari
1 cup cooked garbanzo beans (chickpeas)
½ cup EACH: breadcrumbs (from whole grain bread) and vital wheat gluten
2 tablespoons extra-virgin olive oil
½ teaspoon EACH (dried): rosemary, basil, sage, oregano, and apple cider vinegar
3 cloves garlic, minced or pressed

To make the banzoballs: Preheat your oven to 400 F. Blend the water, tamari, and chickpeas in a food processor or blender until smooth. Remove to a large bowl.

Add the remaining banzoball ingredients (breadcrumbs, gluten, oil, herbs, vinegar, and garlic) to the bean mixture and stir well to combine. Once well combined, knead for a minute or two (either in the bowl or on your countertop). Form into 1-inch balls and place on a lightly oiled baking sheet.

Bake the banzoballs for 10-15 minutes, or until browned on the bottom. Remove and turn over. Bake for another 10-15 minutes, or until the balls are nicely browned on both sides.

Meanwhile, cook the pasta al dente, according to the directions on the package. Drain and set aside. Heat the pasta sauce over low heat until hot.

To serve: Dish up pasta into bowls and then top with sauce and banzoballs. Enjoy!

Serves 6/Green

Pasta with Zesty Lemon White Bean Sauce

This hearty, zippy pasta dish is sure to satisfy! This recipe makes a very generous amount of sauce, which is how it's traditionally served—a nice big portion of bean sauce over a light portion of pasta. However, feel free to customize the proportions so that it's just right for you!

8 oz. whole grain pasta

Sauce:
Two 15 oz. cans white beans (cannellini, northern beans, etc.), drained and rinsed (3 cups beans)
10 large cloves garlic, minced or pressed
½ cup plain, unsweetened nondairy milk
¼ cup fresh lemon juice
1 tablespoon minced lemon zest (the zest of 2 medium-large lemons)
4 teaspoons extra-virgin olive oil
1 teaspoon sea salt
½ teaspoon black pepper

Garnish: 2 tablespoons (packed) fresh basil, cut into thin ribbons

Cook the pasta al dente according to the directions on the package. Drain and set aside.

You'll be able to make the rest of the dish in the time the pasta cooks. Place the drained beans in a medium pot and smash them, using a potato masher. Leave in plenty of texture, but smash them until they've gotten a bit creamy. Add the remaining sauce ingredients and stir well. Heat over medium until thoroughly warmed, about 5 minutes, stirring often. Remove from heat and set aside.

Serve the pasta topped with generous portions of the sauce and sprinkled with the basil.

Serves 4/GF (if using gluten-free pasta)/SF/ Green

	Calories	Saturated fat (g)	Poly unsat fat (g)	Mono unsat fat (g)	Cholesterol (mg)	Sodium (mg)	Potassium (mg)	Carbohydrate (g)	Dietary fiber (g)	Sugars (g)	Protein (g)
PB	476	1.1	1.1	3.6	0	647	133	83	9.2	2.5	18.3
PZLWBS	576	1.1	1.1	3.5	0	580	1080	106	26.8	0.6	24.6

Lemon Ginger Miso Noodles

These delectable noodles are a nutritional powerhouse! Plus, they'll boost your immune system and help detoxify your system. Win!

16 oz. whole grain (or corn-quinoa) pasta

Lemon Ginger Miso Sauce:
5 tablespoons fresh lemon juice
4 tablespoons toasted (dark) sesame oil
3 tablespoons EACH: grated fresh ginger and mellow white miso
2 tablespoons tamari
4 large cloves garlic, pressed or finely minced

Vivacious Veggies:
1 cup shelled edamame, thawed if frozen
1 cup chopped scallions (trimmed and cut into 1-inch pieces)
1 medium carrot (½ cup), finely chopped or julienne cut

Garnish:
½ cup chopped fresh cilantro

Cook the noodles al dente, according to the directions on their package and drain. Set aside.

While the noodles are cooking, place the sauce ingredients in a very large bowl. Combine well using a whisk. Be sure to remove all of the lumps from the miso. Set aside.

Add the noodles and vegetables to the sauce and stir well to combine. Serve topped with cilantro.

Serves 6-8/GF/Blue

Calories	Saturated fat (g)	Poly unsat fat (g)	Mono unsat fat (g)	Cholesterol (mg)	Sodium (mg)	Potassium (mg)	Carbohydrate (g)	Dietary fiber (g)	Sugars (g)	Protein (g)
356	1.2	3.5	3.2	0	577	189	60	6.5	2.2	8.2

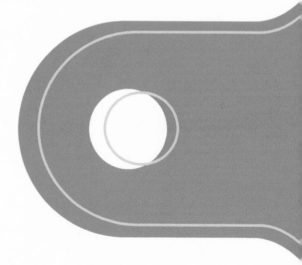

Radiant Rice

Oh, my darling rice. How I love thee! Rice is the perfect staple grain—full of nutrients and highly versatile, rice is perfect in everything from Mexican to Indian to Japanese dishes. Plus, there's just a zen-like simplicity about rice that's grounding and nurturing.

Cilantro Lime Rice

I have had so many versions of this simple, tangy rice and loved them all. I especially like this version, as it is made with whole grain rice and lots of healthy, fresh ingredients! Enjoy.

    1 cup long grain brown rice
    2 cups water
    2 tablespoons EACH: fresh lime juice and finely minced onion (white or yellow)
    ¼ cup (packed) finely chopped fresh cilantro
    1 medium-large clove garlic, minced or pressed
    2 teaspoons oil (coconut, olive, sunflower, or safflower)
    ½ teaspoon sea salt (or less if you prefer)

1. Place the rice and water in a medium sized covered pot and bring to a boil over medium-high heat. Reduce the heat to low and simmer (covered) until the rice is tender and all of the water is absorbed. This should take about 35-45 minutes.

2. Mix all of the remaining ingredients into the rice and stir well to combine. Serve immediately.

Serves 3/GF/SF/Green

You've heard the phrase "Everything in Moderation," but what exactly is moderation? In most of Europe, a woman is labeled as a "heavy" meat-eater when she consumes over 2 ounces of meat per day. Men are labeled heavy consumers of meat at just 3 ounces daily. Africans consume one ounce of meat a day. Asian adults, who are routinely pencil-thin and exceedingly healthy and productive, consume on average less than ½ ounce of meat daily.

Calories	Saturated fat (g)	Poly unsat fat (g)	Mono unsat fat (g)	Cholesterol (mg)	Sodium (mg)	Potassium (mg)	Carbohydrate (g)	Dietary fiber (g)	Sugars (g)	Protein (g)
261	3	0.7	0.8	0	384	172	49.5	2.4	1	5.1

Nori Rolls with Lemon-Lime Soy Dipping Sauce

I have a good friend who flat out hated nori rolls—until she tried these! The secret is the sauce. I also find that people are surprised that they can use brown rice for making sushi. Just be sure to use short grain brown rice, as the other types will not "stick" properly.

    1 cup dry short grain brown rice
    3 cups water

    Lemon Lime Soy Dipping Sauce:
    1 tablespoon EACH: fresh lime juice and fresh lemon juice
    3 tablespoons tamari, shoyu, or soy sauce

    Veggies (Fillin' the Love):
    ½ avocado, peeled and sliced into spears
    1 carrot, julienne sliced or grated
    3 green onions, trimmed and sliced in half lengthwise to form six 3-inch pieces
    1 cup (lightly packed) baby spinach

    Wrap it Up, People:
    3 sheets of nori

    On Hand:
    Large bowl of water
    Sharp knife
    Sushi mat

1. Bring the rice and water to a boil over high heat in a covered pan. Reduce the heat to low and simmer, covered the entire time, until all of the water is absorbed and the rice is tender. Set the rice aside to cool.

2. Prepare your sauce and set it aside. Prepare all of your veggies and set them aside. Prepare yourself to be beside yourself with feelings of accomplishment and tummy love.

3. Now, it's sushi party time! Lay one sheet of nori on the sushi mat, shiny side down.

4. For this next step, you can dip your hands into the bowl of water to prevent the rice from sticking to your hands. Place ⅓ of the rice on the lower half of the nori, using your moistened hands to even the rice out and press it down. Make sure that the rice is evenly distributed over the entire portion of the lower half of the nori. Create a groove across the center of the rice (using the side of your hand) to place the groovy fillings into.

5. Place your desired fillings in the groove and get ready to roll. Using both of your hands, bring the bottom of the mat/nori roll up and over, using your fingers to secure the fillings.

6. Gently (yet firmly) squeeze the mat in order to make sure all of the fillings are stabilized. Roll the rest of the way up. With your finger, spread a little of the water along the edge of the nori. This will seal the edge.

7. Place the nori, seam side down, on a cutting board. Dip your knife into the bowl of water and cut the nori roll across its length into several round pieces. Continue to dip the knife into the water bowl as often as necessary. If your knife remains wet and free of debris, your nori roll pieces will be much neater and less likely to tear.

8. Repeat this process with the remaining nori and fillings. Drizzle the nori pieces with the "Lemon-Lime Soy Sauce" and serve. Drool.

Makes 3 Nori rolls (serves 3 as a main dish or 6 as an appetizer)/GF/Blue

Calories	Saturated fat (g)	Poly unsat fat (g)	Mono unsat fat (g)	Cholesterol (mg)	Sodium (mg)	Potassium (mg)	Carbohydrate (g)	Dietary fiber (g)	Sugars (g)	Protein (g)
315	1.1	1.3	3.9	0	1046	615	56	6.6	2.3	8.9

Caramelized Pineapple, Bean, and Rice Salad

Serve this "salad" with some kale or a tossed green salad for a light and hearty meal.

> 4 cups fresh pineapple chunks (cut into 1-inch chunks)
> 2 cups coarsely chopped onion, white or yellow (chopped into ½-inch pieces)
> 2 teaspoons oil (olive, coconut, or sunflower)
> 2 tablespoons (packed) brown sugar
>
> 2 cups EACH: cooked black beans and cooked rice
> ¼ cup chopped cilantro
> ¼ cup freshly squeezed orange juice
> 2 teaspoons (packed) minced orange zest
> ½ teaspoon sea salt

Preheat your oven to 400 F. Place the pineapple and onion in a large baking pan. Toss with the oil and brown sugar and bake for 45-60 minutes, stirring every 20 minutes, or until the pineapple and onion are golden-browned.

While the pineapple and onion mixture is in the oven, you can get the rest of your dish together. Place all of the remaining ingredients in a large bowl and stir well. Set aside.

When the pineapple and onion are done, add them to the bowl and stir to combine. Serve warm or at room temperature.

Serves 4/GF/SF/Green

Zen Rice

This is one of those dishes that I make frequently and really rely on. It is such the essence of lovely simplicity that I feel like I should be wearing a Zen monk's robe when I eat it! Both children and adults enjoy this dish.

> 1½ cups dry long grain brown rice (or brown basmati rice)
> 3 cups water
> 8 teaspoons oil, optional (coconut or olive)
> 4 teaspoons tamari, shoyu, or soy sauce
> 2 teaspoons nutritional yeast powder

1. Place the rice and water in a rice cooker, pressure cooker, or regular pot with a tight fitting lid. Bring to a boil over high heat. Reduce the heat to low and simmer until the water is absorbed and the rice is tender. In a rice cooker or regular pot, this will take about 45 minutes. In a pressure cooker, this will take about 15 minutes or so once the top begins to shake and shimmy.

2. Once the rice is done, drizzle with the oil and tamari. Sprinkle with the nutritional yeast and serve.

Serves 4-6/GF/Green

Triple Onion Fried Rice

Onion lovers, this dish is for you! With a plethora of onions and garlic in this dish, your immune system will be loving you as much as your taste buds! Please note that this dish does require cooked, cooled rice—hot or warm rice tends to end up getting mushy whereas thoroughly cooled rice retains its texture.

> 4 teaspoons olive oil
> 1 cup finely diced onion, white or yellow
> 1 cup minced shallots
> 4 cups cooked, cooled brown rice
> 1 cup chopped green onion (both white and green parts)
> 4 large cloves garlic, minced or pressed
> 2 tablespoons fresh lemon juice
> 2 teaspoons (packed) minced lemon zest
> ¾ teaspoon sea salt

In a large skillet or wok, heat the olive oil over medium heat. Add the diced onion and shallots and stir-fry for about 5 minutes, or until the onions are nicely browned.

Add the rice, green onion, and garlic to the onions and stir well. Stir-fry for another 1-2 minutes.

Stir the lemon juice, zest, and salt into the mixture until thoroughly combined. Serve.

Serves 4/GF/SF/Green

	Calories	Saturated fat (g)	Poly unsat fat (g)	Mono unsat fat (g)	Cholesterol (mg)	Sodium (mg)	Potassium (mg)	Carbohydrate (g)	Dietary fiber (g)	Sugars (g)	Protein (g)
CPBRS	417	2.3	0.6	0.5	0	289	771	88	13.1	37.2	11.8
ZR	274	6.6	0.7	1	0	277	157	43.5	2.3	0.6	5.5
TOFR	315	1	1.1	3.9	0	432	397	59	4.7	2.8	6.4

Japanese Ume Rice

You may have never even heard of umeboshi before, but I encourage you to give this a try. Umeboshi plum assists digestion, improves blood quality, and is alkalinizing and detoxifying—not to mention delicious!

1 cup rice (you may use any kind of brown rice or forbidden black rice)
2 cups water
1 tablespoon umeboshi (ume plum) vinegar
4 teaspoons fresh lime juice
1 tablespoon toasted sesame oil
1 teaspoon umeboshi plum paste

Add last:
¼ cup EACH: Finely chopped red cabbage, grated carrot, minced white onion, and minced green onions

1. Place the rice and water in a medium pot with a tight-fitting lid. Bring to a boil over high heat, then reduce heat to low and simmer until all of the water is absorbed and the rice is tender. Set aside to cool.

2. In a large bowl, combine the ume vinegar, lime juice, sesame oil, and plum paste. Whisk until smooth. Add the rice and vegetables and stir until well combined. Serve at room temperature or cold. Do not reheat.

Serves 4/GF/SF/Green

Go Wild Rice Pilaf

This simple pilaf is like a warm hug on a cold day—yes, you're loved!

1 cup wild rice
2½ cups water*
½ cup diced onion
1 cup peas (shelled, fresh or frozen)
½ cup finely chopped fresh parsley
¼ cup Chicky Baby Seasoning (p. 16)
3 large cloves garlic, minced or pressed
1½ teaspoons extra-virgin olive oil
½ teaspoon sea salt

In a pot with a tight-fitting lid, place the wild rice, water, and onion. Cover and bring to a boil over high heat. Reduce heat to low and simmer for 45 minutes, or until all of the water is absorbed and the rice is tender.*

Remove from heat and immediately stir in the peas and cover for a minute, or until the peas are warmed through.

Stir in the remaining ingredients and serve.

Serves 2-4/GF/SF/Green

*Note: Friends, I wish I could give you an accurate amount of water for this dish that would work every time, under every circumstance. However, wild rice is in fact wild. It's unpredictable. It's ka-razy. Depending on the type of wild rice you buy (and a few other factors), you may need different amounts of water here. Here's what I recommend: Begin with the suggested amount of water. Once the rice is tender, if you have extra water, pour it off (or save it for stock). Alternatively, if you need more water, just add a bit more as it cooks. It may seem like wild rice is just too wild to bother with, but trust me—it's worth it!

	Calories	Saturated fat (g)	Poly unsat fat (g)	Mono unsat fat (g)	Cholesterol (mg)	Sodium (mg)	Potassium (mg)	Carbohydrate (g)	Dietary fiber (g)	Sugars (g)	Protein (g)
JUR	214	0.8	1.9	1.8	0	930	204	38.7	2.2	1.2	3.9
GWRP	307	0.5	0.8	1.9	0	1261	640	55	9	5.7	16

Fast and Forbidden Fried Rice

If you have cooked rice on hand, this dish will come together in a lickety smack. And for all you cuteness junkies out there, you'll be happy to know that it's extremely colorful too, due to the brilliant and nutrient-rich ingredients.

1 cup forbidden rice (black rice)
2 cups water
2 tablespoons sesame seeds
1 tablespoon EACH: non-virgin coconut oil and toasted sesame oil
2 tablespoons tamari
¾ cup scallions (trimmed and cut into ½-inch pieces on the diagonal)
Medium carrot, diced
½ cup shelled edamame
1 tablespoon minced fresh ginger
2 large cloves garlic, pressed

1. Place the rice and water in a covered pot and bring to a boil over high heat. Reduce heat to low and simmer until the rice is tender and all of the water has been absorbed. Let the rice cool in the fridge for at least an hour (to prevent mushy fried rice).

2. In a wok or large skillet, heat the sesame seeds and oils over medium-high heat. Stir well and cook for one minute.

3. Add the tamari, scallions, carrot, edamame, ginger, and cooled rice and stir well to combine. Cook for 2-3 minutes, stirring often. Stir in the garlic until well combined. Say "stir" a few more times. Remove from heat and serve.

Serves 4/GF/Green

Simple Sesame Miso Rice

This is one of those ridiculously simple dishes that's oddly satisfying – perfect for lazy days!

4 cups cooked, warm brown rice (any variety)
¼ cup chopped chives or green onions

Simple Sesame Miso Sauce:
3 tablespoons EACH: raw tahini and mellow white miso (do not use dark miso here)
2 tablespoons dried onion granules
½ cup warm water

Whisk the ingredients for the sauce together until smooth.

Serve the sauce over the rice and top with chives or green onions.

Serves 4/GF/Green

Comforting Chicky Rice

This recipe couldn't be simpler, and the name says it all. I've purposely simplified this recipe so that it can be easily multiplied to serve any number of people. Enjoy this warm, nourishing food hug!

1 cup cooked brown rice, warm or hot
2 teaspoons Chicky Baby Seasoning (p. 16)
1 teaspoon olive oil
1 clove garlic, minced or pressed

Stir all of the ingredients together and serve.

Serves 1/GF/SF/Green

	Calories	Saturated fat (g)	Poly unsat fat (g)	Mono unsat fat (g)	Cholesterol (mg)	Sodium (mg)	Potassium (mg)	Carbohydrate (g)	Dietary fiber (g)	Sugars (g)	Protein (g)
FFFR	272	3.8	2.5	2.4	0	521	327	38.4	4.3	2.7	8.2
SSMR	321	1.2	3.4	2.8	0	496	271	55	5.9	1.1	8.5
CCR	282	1	1.1	3.9	0	437	259	49	4.8	0.2	7.1

Pineapple Rice

This dish was inspired by a local Thai café that serves a delicious pineapple rice—although theirs is topped with salted, roasted cashews. Either way, it's a simple, satisfying dish!

   2½ cups cooked long grain brown rice, completely cooled
   1½ cups pineapple chunks
   4 teaspoons tamari, soy sauce, or shoyu
   2 teaspoons oil (toasted sesame, sunflower, or coconut)
   ½ cup minced green onions
   1/3 cup julienne-cut carrots (or diced carrots)
   2 tablespoons minced onion (white or yellow)

In a large skillet or wok, combine all of the ingredients over medium-high heat.

Stir-fry for about 5 minutes, or until all of the ingredients are hot and thoroughly combined. Serve warm.

   Serves about 3/GF/Green

Population studies show that when people migrate from one country to another, they acquire the cancer rate of the country in which they live, even though their genetic makeup hasn't changed. This strongly indicates that the vast majority of cancer is the result of diet and lifestyle, not genes.

Calories	Saturated fat (g)	Poly unsat fat (g)	Mono unsat fat (g)	Cholesterol (mg)	Sodium (mg)	Potassium (mg)	Carbohydrate (g)	Dietary fiber (g)	Sugars (g)	Protein (g)
278	0.7	1.8	1.7	0	468	273	55	4.9	15.2	5.8

Veggie Rice Bowl with Ginger Pineapple Sauce

This pretty dish combines enzyme-rich raw vegetables with rice and steamed broccoli for a new twist on stir-fry. In my household, we make up a double batch of the sauce and then make up individual servings throughout the week whenever the craving hits! However, if you'll be serving the whole dish at once, multiply the rice and vegetables by four.

Chef's note: If you don't mind bold flavors, add the lime juice, garlic, and ginger to the sauce after you've removed it from heat. You'll get more vitamins and enzymes from those superfoods that way!

Ginger Pineapple Sauce:
20 oz. can pineapple tidbits (in their own juice, no sugar or other additives)
¼ cup agave nectar
3 tablespoons fresh lime juice
2 tablespoons grated fresh ginger (note: only use half the ginger if you prefer a mild flavor)
2 tablespoons tamari
1 tablespoon EACH: tomato paste and apple cider vinegar
2 medium cloves garlic, minced or pressed
2 tablespoons EACH: arrowroot and water

For Each Serving:
1 cup cooked, warm brown rice
1 cup warm steamed broccoli (crisp-tender and bright green)
1 cup baby spinach
¾ cup finely chopped red cabbage
¼ cup grated or julienne-cut carrot

1. Have your rice and vegetables ready to go, as the sauce will come together quickly.

2. To make the sauce: Combine the pineapple (juice and all), agave, lime juice, ginger, tamari, tomato paste, vinegar, and garlic in a medium pot. Stir well.

3. In a small dish, stir the arrowroot into the water until smooth and no longer lumpy. Add the mixture to the sauce and whisk well. Heat the sauce over medium heat, whisking often, until thickened. This should only take about 5 minutes.

4. To serve: Place the baby spinach in a large bowl and top with the rice. Sprinkle with the broccoli, cabbage, and carrot. Finish with about ¾ cup of sauce.

82

Serves 4 (the sauce serves 4)/GF/Green

Calories	Saturated fat (g)	Poly unsat fat (g)	Mono unsat fat (g)	Cholesterol (mg)	Sodium (mg)	Potassium (mg)	Carbohydrate (g)	Dietary fiber (g)	Sugars (g)	Protein (g)
480	0.5	1	0.7	0	626	1185	108	13	42	12

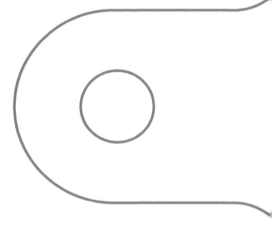

Gorgeous Grains

Here's your chance to enjoy the filling, low-fat, nutrient-dense whole grains that everyone craves. When you prepare them the Get Waisted way, you'll have no problem sliding into those skinny jeans and functioning at full sexiness capacity!

Perfect Tabouli

Unlike many tabouli salads that tend to be on the bland side, this one has flavor for days. Plus, with all of the detoxifying, vitalizing, alkalinizing ingredients, this delicious salad will make you look like a movie star—and a photoshopped one at that!

1 cup bulgur wheat
1½ cups water
¾ cup diced cucumber
3 cups minced fresh curly parsley
¼ cup minced fresh mint
½ cup minced onion, white or yellow
¼ cup plus 2 tablespoons fresh lemon juice
2 tablespoons extra-virgin olive oil
¾ teaspoon sea salt

1. Bring the bulgur and water to a boil in a covered pot, then remove from heat. Allow to sit, covered tightly, until all of the water is absorbed and the bulgur is tender (about an hour). Fluff with a fork and set aside to cool, uncovered.

2. Stir all of the remaining ingredients together in a large bowl. Add the bulgur and stir well to mix. Viola! The perfect tabouli has now become your immediate present-moment reality. Be here; chow.

Serves about 4/SF/Green

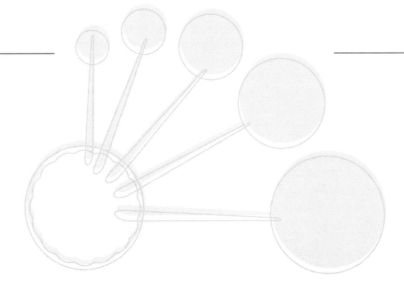

25% of turkey and chicken sold in Detroit, Michigan supermarkets was found to be contaminated with multi-drug resistant bacteria in a study in 2010. In the U.S., we use 80% of our antibiotics on farm animals being raised for food.

Calories	Saturated fat (g)	Poly unsat fat (g)	Mono unsat fat (g)	Cholesterol (mg)	Sodium (mg)	Potassium (mg)	Carbohydrate (g)	Dietary fiber (g)	Sugars (g)	Protein (g)
192	1.1	0.8	5.1	0	450	351	27	5.2	2.9	7.1

Sonoran Enchiladas

In my mother-in-law's Mexican hometown, there's a tradition every August. Everyone makes their own version of these and people go from house to house trying all the different kinds. This uber-simple version has always been one of my husband's favorites, and it comes together in a flash if you have cooked potatoes on hand!

1 medium potato, baked, cooled, and peeled
½ teaspoon olive oil
2 green onions, trimmed and chopped (½ cup chopped green onions)
1 large clove garlic, minced or pressed

1 corn tortilla
½ cup prepared enchilada sauce (I recommend the Simply Organic brand)
1 teaspoon nutritional yeast
2 tablespoons finely chopped red cabbage

1. Cut the potato into ½-inch chunks and place in a medium skillet. Toss with the ½ teaspoon oil and pan-fry over medium-high heat for about 4 minutes. Add the green onions and garlic and pan-fry for another minute or so. If desired, season with a little salt and pepper—although you may wish to omit them as the enchilada sauce will add a lot of flavor.

2. Heat the enchilada sauce until thoroughly warmed. Next, warm the tortilla by placing it in a dry skillet for a minute or less. Place the tortilla on a plate.

3. Top the warm tortilla with the potato-onion mixture and cover with the sauce. Sprinkle with the nutritional yeast and top with the cabbage. Enjoy!

Serves 1/GF/SF/Green

Asparagus Walnut Quinoa Salad

This dish has it all – crunchy veggies, hearty quinoa, omega-rich walnuts, and a delectable dressing! You're welcome.

Maple Mustard Dressing:
6 tablespoons prepared yellow mustard
¼ cup pure maple syrup
2 tablespoons EACH: water and extra-virgin olive oil
2 teaspoons EACH: tamari and apple cider vinegar

Salad:
4 cups cooked quinoa
4 cups asparagus, trimmed and chopped into 2-inch pieces
9 cups baby greens
½ cup thinly sliced onion, white or yellow
6 tablespoons raw walnut pieces

1. Prepare the dressing and set it aside.

2. Steam the asparagus for 3-5 minutes, or until bright green and crisp-tender. Remove from heat and set aside.

3. Meanwhile, place the quinoa, greens, and onions in bowls. Top with the steamed asparagus and walnuts. Drizzle with the dressing and serve immediately. Yum!

Serves 4/GF/Green

What we eat, individually and as a member of our global community, has an impact far beyond our waistlines and cholesterol panels. Wastefulness in food production is impacting the availability of our precious natural resources, increasing our reliance on foreign oil production, and contributing to climate change. The production of animal protein requires plenty of energy. Each calorie of meat protein takes 28 calories of energy to produce. In contrast, each calorie of grain protein takes only 3.3 calories to produce. Grain has to be grown and transported, but instead of using that grain protein to feed a person, it is used instead to feed the farm animals at multiple meals for several months. The animal is slaughtered, packaged, transported, and refrigerated. That means that a 328-calorie, six-ounce filet mignon, requires 9,184 calories to be produced. In contrast, a 400-calorie, two-cup portion of brown rice only takes 1320 calories of energy to produce. By switching to a meatless dinner, a family of four will save 31,456 calories of energy at just one meal.

Are you working hard at energy conservation by shutting off the lights when no one is in the room? Shutting off a lightbulb saves just 1376 calories each day. By serving just one meatless meal to your family, you will save the energy equivalent of shutting off 23 lights for a whole day.

	Calories	Saturated fat (g)	Poly unsat fat (g)	Mono unsat fat (g)	Cholesterol (mg)	Sodium (mg)	Potassium (mg)	Carbohydrate (g)	Dietary fiber (g)	Sugars (g)	Protein (g)
SE	278	0.5	0.6	1.8	0	1064	768	56	7	12	8.2
AWQS	502	1.8	6.2	6.6	0	485	740	71	14.3	20.2	16.5

Mexican Polenta Bowl

This easy peasy dish is the epitome of Mexican comfort food. Creamy polenta is topped with all kinds of spicy, healthy goodies for a light, colorful, and satisfying entrée.

Polenta:
¾ cup dry polenta
3 cups water
3 tablespoons nutritional yeast
¾ teaspoon sea salt
3 medium-large cloves garlic, minced or pressed

Toppings:
Medium tomato, chopped
½ cup cooked black beans
¼ cup EACH: diced green onions and chopped cilantro
½ medium avocado, chopped

Optional:
2 tablespoons minced jalapeno
½ fresh lime

Prepare all of the toppings and set them aside.

In a medium-large pot, place the polenta and water. Set to medium-high heat and bring to a boil, stirring with a wire whisk. Reduce heat to low and continue to whisk often until the polenta is thick. This should take about ten minutes.

Place the polenta in two bowls and top with the tomato, beans, onions, cilantro, and avocado. If desired, add the jalapeno and squeeze with lime juice. Serve.

Serves 2/GF/SF/Green

Calories	Saturated fat (g)	Poly unsat fat (g)	Mono unsat fat (g)	Cholesterol (mg)	Sodium (mg)	Potassium (mg)	Carbohydrate (g)	Dietary fiber (g)	Sugars (g)	Protein (g)
427	1.3	1.5	5.2	0	869	944	71	13.7	3.8	17

Roasted Tomato and Garlic Quinoa

I created this dish last summer when I had an abundance of juicy, perfect tomatoes. I was actually really surprised at how delicious this simple treatment of them was! You can also serve the juicy tomato mixture over whole grain pasta or just plain in a bowl.

    8 medium tomatoes (stems removed)
    10 cloves of garlic (unpeeled)
    1 tablespoon extra-virgin olive oil
    Truffle salt to taste (or sea salt)
    2 cups cooked quinoa

Preheat your oven to 350 F.

Place the tomatoes and garlic on a baking sheet and drizzle with the oil. Shake the pan to distribute the oil evenly onto the tomatoes and garlic. Bake for about an hour, or until it all looks and smells unbearably gooey and delicious.

Take out of the oven. Remove the peels from the garlic and serve the mixture over the cooked quinoa. Sprinkle with the salt and serve.

Serves 2/GF/SF/Green

Calories	Saturated fat (g)	Poly unsat fat (g)	Mono unsat fat (g)	Cholesterol (mg)	Sodium (mg)	Potassium (mg)	Carbohydrate (g)	Dietary fiber (g)	Sugars (g)	Protein (g)
393	1.2	1.2	5.2	0	164	1544	64	11.4	13.1	13.4

Asian Vegetable Pancakes with Shoyu Lime Sauce

Pancakes for dinner? Of course—why would you even think of denying yourself this basic human right?

> 2 tablespoons ground flax (flaxmeal)
> 1¾ cup nondairy milk, plain and unsweetened
> 1 cup whole-wheat pastry flour
> ½ teaspoon turmeric
> ¼ teaspoon sea salt
> 1 teaspoon baking powder
> ½ teaspoon baking soda
> ½ cup EACH: minced green onions, thinly sliced or chopped shiitake mushrooms, minced white onion, and grated carrot

> **Shoyu Lime Sauce:**
> 2 tablespoons shoyu (or tamari)
> 2 tablespoons fresh lime juice

Stir the sauce ingredients together and set aside.

In a medium bowl, whisk the flaxmeal with the milk. Set aside for 5 minutes and then whisk again.

Add the flour, turmeric, and salt to the mixture and whisk well to thoroughly combine. Add the baking powder and soda and whisk again. Add the vegetables to the batter and stir or whisk well.

Heat a large skillet over medium-high heat and spray lightly with oil. Pour the batter onto the hot skillet in pancake-type formations. When the bottom is browned, flip over. When both sides are browned, remove to a plate. This should take about 1-2 minutes on each side.

Continue to cook the pancakes in batches until all of the batter is gone.

Serve the pancakes hot or warm with the sauce for dipping. Yum!

> Serves 2/Green

Calories	Saturated fat (g)	Poly unsat fat (g)	Mono unsat fat (g)	Cholesterol (mg)	Sodium (mg)	Potassium (mg)	Carbohydrate (g)	Dietary fiber (g)	Sugars (g)	Protein (g)
380	0.8	2.2	0.6	0	1946	610	66	13.8	5.5	18.9

Raw Moroccan Quinoa Spinach Toss

Although this dish requires overnight soaking, it'll come together in a snap the next day. And it's worth it! Not only is it fat-free, raw, and incredibly nourishing, it's also super flavorful!

1 cup dry quinoa

Sweet-Savory Sauce:
1 teaspoon EACH: ground cumin and minced organic orange zest
¾ cup fresh squeezed orange juice
4 teaspoons EACH: fresh lemon juice and very finely minced onion
2 teaspoons ground cinnamon
2 tablespoons raw agave nectar

Simple Salad:
½ cup raisins
1 cup (packed) baby spinach, cut into very thin ribbons or minced
1½ tablespoons fresh mint, minced

Place the quinoa in plenty of water to cover (about 3 cups water) and set aside for 6-12 hours. Drain the quinoa well and set aside.

Stir the sauce ingredients together in a medium-sized bowl until well combined. Add the quinoa, raisins, and spinach to the sauce and toss to thoroughly combine.

Allow the mixture to marinate for at least 20 minutes, stirring occasionally to saturate the sauce into everything. If you have the time to marinate this for an hour, that's even better. Toss and serve. If you have leftovers, this will keep for a few days in an airtight container, refrigerated.

Serves 4/GF/SF/Green

	Calories	Saturated fat (g)	Poly unsat fat (g)	Mono unsat fat (g)	Cholesterol (mg)	Sodium (mg)	Potassium (mg)	Carbohydrate (g)	Dietary fiber (g)	Sugars (g)	Protein (g)
RMQST	279	0.3	1.5	0.8	0	12.2	559	59	4.9	24.4	7.4
BSCO	512	1	0	0	0	33.6	342	94	10.8	25	17.5
QTB	229	0.7	2.1	2.5	0	37.2	395	37.8	4.8	6.8	7.4

British Steel Cut Oats

My daughter's English nana got our family hooked on this interesting twist on oats. The steel cut version is heartier than regular rolled oats and adds a nice texture. Even though this couldn't be simpler, it's addictively delicious and nourishing.

> 1 cup steel cut oats
> 2¼ cups water
> 1 cup nondairy vanilla yogurt (I recommend Amande almond yogurt or Nancy's soy yogurt)
> 3 tablespoons apricot fruit spread (fruit-sweetened jam)

1. In a medium pot, place the oats and water. Bring to a boil over high heat. Reduce heat to low and simmer for about 20-30 minutes, stirring occasionally, until the oats are tender and the water has been absorbed.

2. Serve the oats topped with the yogurt and a dollop of fruit spread.

Serves 2/GF/SF/Green

Quinoa Treasures Bowl

Nutritious, fresh, and easy to make—now that's what I'm talking about!

Quinoa:
1 cup dry quinoa, rinsed and drained
2 cups water, preferably filtered

Treasures:
The segments and minced zest of 1 large organic orange
2 tablespoons EACH: raisins and sliced kalamata olives
3–4 tablespoons minced red onion
1 teaspoon EACH: fresh lemon juice and extra virgin olive oil
¼ teaspoon sea salt

Optional Flair: 2 tablespoons shelled pistachios, whole or crushed

1. Bring the quinoa and water to a boil in a covered pot. Reduce heat to low and simmer (partially covered) until all of the water has been absorbed—this will usually take about 15 minutes.

2. Toss the quinoa with all of the treasures and stir well to combine. If desired, top with some pistachios. Serve immediately or refrigerate for up to two days.

Serves 4/SF/GF/Green

Double Garlic Quinoa

Garlic likers, move on. There's nothing to see here. Garlic lovers, we should form a gang. We'll serve this at our potlucks.

> 1 cup whole quinoa
> 2 cups water
> 6 large cloves garlic, peeled and thinly sliced
> 1 tablespoon extra-virgin olive oil
> 3 medium cloves garlic, minced or pressed
> 1 tablespoon EACH: minced fresh parsley and minced fresh basil (both very well packed)
> Sea salt and freshly ground pepper to taste

Rinse the quinoa in a fine mesh strainer and drain well. Place in a pot with the water. Cover and bring to a boil over medium-high heat. Reduce heat to low and simmer until all of the water has been absorbed, about 15 minutes.

While the quinoa is cooking, you can get all of the other ingredients ready. First, place the sliced garlic and olive oil in a small skillet over medium heat. Once it begins to sizzle, turn the heat down to medium-low and stir often. As soon as the garlic turns a beautiful shade of golden-brown, remove from heat. If you wait too long, the garlic will over-brown and become bitter.

Place the cooked quinoa in a large bowl and add the garlic-oil mixture. I like to use a rubber spatula to scrape all of the goodness out of the pan and into the quinoa, as it makes a difference in how the end product tastes.

Add all of the remaining ingredients, including the salt and pepper to taste. Toss gently with a spoon and serve. This will keep for several days, refrigerated in an airtight container. Buh-bye vampires!

Serves 3/GF/SF/Green

Calories	Saturated fat (g)	Poly unsat fat (g)	Mono unsat fat (g)	Cholesterol (mg)	Sodium (mg)	Potassium (mg)	Carbohydrate (g)	Dietary fiber (g)	Sugars (g)	Protein (g)
263	1.1	2.4	4.3	0	93	369	39.6	4.3	0.1	8.7

When you consider that a serving of California beef takes 5127 gallons of water to produce, and a serving of grain only 300 gallons, you realize something amazing. If a family of four gives up meat at dinner each night, they would conserve enough water to fill an Olympic-sized swimming pool in just 55 days.

Cheesy Broccoli Baked Potato

Baked potatoes as an entrée? Why yes! Potatoes have unfairly gotten a bad rap in the weight loss arena, but in reality there are few more perfect foods. Potatoes are filling, fiber-rich, extremely high in potassium, fat-free, and full of vitamins and minerals. If you keep the cheesy mix on hand, this will become a favorite easy go-to meal—or at least that's what plays out in our house!

4 large potatoes, scrubbed (skins on)
6 cups broccoli, cut into bite-size pieces

Cheesy Mix:
1 cup raw cashews
1¼ cups nutritional yeast
½ cup rolled oats
¼ cup arrowroot
2 tablespoons EACH: seasoned salt and garlic granules (granulated garlic)
1½ tablespoons onion granules (granulated onion)
½ teaspoon ground turmeric

Preheat your oven to 400 F. Place the potatoes in the oven (just right onto the racks is fine). Bake for about 45 minutes, or until tender.

While the potatoes are baking, you can assemble the rest of your dish. First, place all of the ingredients for the cheesy mix in a food processor. Blend until a fine powder. This cheesy mix will store in the fridge (in an airtight container) for months—although it never lasts that long in our house! Set it aside.

When the potatoes are almost tender, steam the broccoli until tender and bright green. Set aside.

Place 1 cup of cheesy mix with 2 cups water in a small pot, set to medium heat (it's a 2:1 ratio, water to mix). Whisking often, cook until thickened. This will take well under five minutes.

To assemble: Place the baked potatoes on plates, cut them open, and mash them. Top with some broccoli and pour a generous serving of the sauce on top. Enjoy!

Serves 4/GF/SF/Green

Calories	Saturated fat (g)	Poly unsat fat (g)	Mono unsat fat (g)	Cholesterol (mg)	Sodium (mg)	Potassium (mg)	Carbohydrate (g)	Dietary fiber (g)	Sugars (g)	Protein (g)
730	2.5	2.7	7	0	2371	3100	114	24.8	7.3	41.4

Lemon Asparagus Quinoa

The first time I tried this dish, I may or may not have cursed loudly under my breath. I was just that taken by the lemony deliciousness. However, this tends to be much better when it's first made—if you have leftovers, you may want to add a bit more lemon to freshen them up. Enjoy!

2 cups asparagus, trimmed and cut into 1-inch pieces
1 teaspoon extra-virgin olive oil
½ cup dry quinoa
1 cup water
1 tablespoon EACH: fresh lemon juice and additional extra-virgin olive oil
1 teaspoon (packed) minced lemon zest (zest of about one large lemon)
2 medium-large cloves garlic, minced or pressed
¼ teaspoon EACH: sea salt and black pepper

1. Preheat the oven to 400° F. Place the asparagus on a baking sheet and drizzle with the 1 teaspoon of oil. Shake the pan to coat the asparagus with the oil. Bake for 10 minutes. Remove from the oven and shake the pan again (to turn the asparagus). Bake for another 10 minutes, or until the asparagus is tender and roasted.

2. Meanwhile, place the quinoa and water in a covered pot and bring to a boil over high heat. Reduce heat to low and simmer until the water has been absorbed and the quinoa is tender, about 15 minutes.

3. While the asparagus and quinoa are doing their thang, you can get your groove on with the rest of this dish. In a medium bowl, place the remaining ingredients and stir well. Add the asparagus and quinoa to the bowl and stir everything together well. Serve warm, at room temperature, or cold.

Serves 2/GF/SF/Green

Calories	Saturated fat (g)	Poly unsat fat (g)	Mono unsat fat (g)	Cholesterol (mg)	Sodium (mg)	Potassium (mg)	Carbohydrate (g)	Dietary fiber (g)	Sugars (g)	Protein (g)
271	1.7	2.5	7.4	0	289	538	34.4	6.1	2.8	9.2

Carl's Calabasitas

My husband Carl has perfected the art of this nutritious, traditional Mexican dish. It's amazing to me that something so simple and light can be so addictively fabulous! When zucchini is in season, Calabasitas are on the menu every other day, and he's the one cooking them up. Lucky me!

½ cup diced onion, white or yellow
1 teaspoon olive oil
5 cups diced zucchini (cut into ¼-inch cubes)
4 large garlic cloves, peeled and roughly chopped
¼ teaspoon sea salt
½ teaspoon pepper
½ cup fresh salsa, your choice
2 tablespoons fresh lime juice
8 corn tortillas
¼ cup fresh cilantro

In a large skillet, sauté the onion in the oil for one minute over medium heat.
Next, add the zucchini and stir. Allow to cook over medium heat for five minutes without stirring. Then add the garlic, salt, and pepper and stir well. Cook for another five minutes without stirring.
Stir again and let cook for five more minutes (don't stir during this time). Yes, there is a lot of non-stirring going on here—Carl swears by it!
Add the salsa and stir. Cook for another five minutes and remove from heat. Cool for a minute and stir in the lime juice. Set aside.
To prepare the tortillas: Dip or rinse the tortillas in water and then place them in a single layer in a large skillet over medium heat. (You may have to do this in a few batches.) Cover and cook for one minute, flipping the tortilla midway (cook for 30 seconds on each side). Remove from the skillet and fill with a little of the zucchini mixture. Garnish with cilantro and fold up like a soft taco to serve.

Serves 2-4/GF/SF/Green

Calories	Saturated fat (g)	Poly unsat fat (g)	Mono unsat fat (g)	Cholesterol (mg)	Sodium (mg)	Potassium (mg)	Carbohydrate (g)	Dietary fiber (g)	Sugars (g)	Protein (g)
191	0.6	1.1	1.5	0	489	841	36.7	6.7	8.3	6.7

Chili Lime Popcorn

Yes, you heard me right. Popcorn. Silly as it sounds, I love having popcorn as an entrée! It's actually quite legitimate, folks—popcorn is a whole grain, and without gobs of butter it's actually low in fat, high in fiber, and nutritious! This particular popcorn dish is not only crazy flavorful, it's also super immune-boosting!

½ cup popcorn
1 tablespoon oil (sunflower, coconut, or olive)
1 tablespoon nutritional yeast
1 teaspoon minced lime zest
½ teaspoon sea salt
¼ teaspoon EACH: ground cayenne powder and garlic granules (granulated garlic)
3 tablespoons fresh lime juice

Set a large pot (with a tight fitting lid) to medium-high heat and add the oil and popcorn. To pop, shake very often and remove from heat immediately once the popping slows down to 1-2 seconds between pops.

Remove the popcorn to a very large bowl. Sprinkle with the yeast, lime zest, salt, cayenne, and garlic.

You'll add the lime juice last—it provides a nice wet base so that all of the seasonings stick without having to use more oil. Stir very well and serve. Enjoy your movie!

Serves 2/GF/Green

Green Goodness Quinoa

This dish is based on my all-time favorite green vegetables, especially the ones that taste amazing when roasted. What is it about roasting vegetables that makes them so luscious and enticing? Actually, I don't even care—just give me a bowl of this and I'll stop with all the questions and just eat.

Green Goodness:
2 cups asparagus, cut into 1-inch pieces
Medium zucchini, chopped into small pieces (1½ cups chopped zucchini)
1 cup chopped green onion (both white and green parts, cut into 1-inch pieces)
1 cup (lightly packed) kale, stems removed and cut into ribbons
6 large garlic cloves, peeled and roughly chopped
1 tablespoon olive oil
½ teaspoon EACH: garlic granules, seasoned salt, and black pepper

Quinoa
1 cup dry quinoa
2 cups water
1 tablespoon fresh lemon juice
¼ teaspoon sea salt

Preheat the oven to 400 F.

Place the vegetables in a large bowl along with the chopped garlic, oil, garlic granules, seasoned salt, and pepper. Toss well with a spoon or spatula. Place on a large baking sheet and bake for 10 minutes. Remove from the oven, stir well, and bake for another 10 minutes, or until tender and nicely browned. Remove from the oven and set aside.

While the veggies are roasting, you can get the quinoa ready. Place the quinoa and water in a medium pot with a tight-fitting lid. Bring to a boil over high heat. Reduce heat to low and simmer until the quinoa is tender and all of the water has been absorbed. Remove from heat and toss with the lemon juice and sea salt.

To serve: place the quinoa in bowls and top with the roasted vegetables. Enjoy—and please feel free to invite me over to share!

Serves 2/GF/SF/Green

	Calories	Saturated fat (g)	Poly unsat fat (g)	Mono unsat fat (g)	Cholesterol (mg)	Sodium (mg)	Potassium (mg)	Carbohydrate (g)	Dietary fiber (g)	Sugars (g)	Protein (g)
CLP	103	5.9	0.2	0.4	0	506	168	7.9	1.9	0.8	4
GGQ	461	1.7	3.8	6.3	0	704	1275	73	11.5	7	18.4

Rosemary Polenta with Mushrooms

Think of this as quick, nourishing comfort food that will keep you trim and energized!

Rosemary Polenta:
1 cup dry polenta
3 cups water
1 teaspoon dried rosemary
¼ cup nutritional yeast
½ teaspoon sea salt

Mushrooms:
8 oz. baby portabellas (3 cups sliced portabellas)
4 teaspoons balsamic vinegar
1 tablespoon tamari
1 teaspoon extra-virgin olive oil
3 large cloves garlic, minced or pressed

1. In a medium pot, place the polenta, water, and rosemary. Bring to a boil over high heat. Reduce heat to as low as possible and continue to cook, whisking often (with a wire whisk) until the mixture is thick. This will take about 10 minutes.

2. In a large skillet, place the portabellas, vinegar, tamari, and oil over medium-high heat. Sauté for about 5 minutes, stirring often, until the mushrooms are very tender and all of the liquids have been absorbed. Stir in the garlic and set aside.

3. Serve the polenta topped with the mushrooms.

Serves 3/GF/Green

Calories	Saturated fat (g)	Poly unsat fat (g)	Mono unsat fat (g)	Cholesterol (mg)	Sodium (mg)	Potassium (mg)	Carbohydrate (g)	Dietary fiber (g)	Sugars (g)	Protein (g)
281	0.4	0.7	1.3	0	732	608	51	6.1	4	12.3

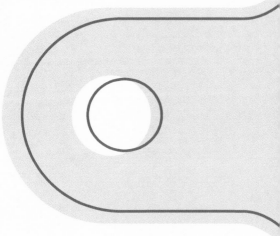

Slimming Soups

Bowl of love, anyone? Plant-based soups are not only nurturing and soothing, they're also perfect for trimming down and getting ultra fit! Soups are the perfect vehicle for all sorts of superfoods, too—miso, garlic, ginger, and kale all make their appearance in this star-studded chapter!

Get Skinny Soup

This is the perfect soup for weight loss, as it's very low in fat and calories, extremely high in fiber, and oddly satisfying!

1 medium carrot, thinly sliced
1 medium stalk of celery, thinly sliced
¾ cup finely chopped onion (one small-medium sized onion)
1 tablespoon extra virgin olive oil
7 cups water, preferably filtered
2 cups chopped green cabbage
1 cup dry lentils (green or brown), rinsed well and sorted
One 14.5 oz. can diced tomatoes with garlic and onions (juice and all)
1½ teaspoons EACH: dried oregano and agave nectar
2 bay leaves
3-inch piece kombu
1 teaspoon sea salt
Lots of freshly ground black pepper, to taste (I use about ¾ teaspoon)
½ teaspoon balsamic vinegar
3-5 medium cloves garlic, pressed or minced

Garnish: 16 basil leaves, cut into thin ribbons

1. In a large soup pot, sauté the carrot, celery, and onion in the oil over medium-high heat for about 5 minutes, or until the veggies begin to soften.

2. Add the water, cabbage, lentils, tomatoes, oregano, agave, bay leaves, and kombu. Bring to a boil over high heat. Reduce heat to low and simmer, partially covered, until the lentils are soft. This will take about an hour.

3. Once the lentils are tender, remove the bay leaves and kombu. Stir in the remaining items (salt, pepper, vinegar, and garlic). Ladle into bowls and garnish with the basil. This will store refrigerated for up to ten days.

Serves 6/GF/SF/Green

Calories	Saturated fat (g)	Poly unsat fat (g)	Mono unsat fat (g)	Cholesterol (mg)	Sodium (mg)	Potassium (mg)	Carbohydrate (g)	Dietary fiber (g)	Sugars (g)	Protein (g)
182	0.4	0.5	1.8	0	600	542	30.2	12.5	6.6	9.8

Hearty Vegan Chili

This hearty chili is filling, delicious, and extremely flavorful. Plus, it's perfect for fooling carnivores into thinking they're eating meat-based chili. Shh...

2 tablespoons olive oil
2 small-medium onions, chopped
2 cups crumbled tempeh (crumble any kind of tempeh)
2 cups liquid vegetarian broth (vegetable or vegetarian "chicken")
2 cans (15 oz. each) red kidney or pinto beans, with juice (not drained)
2 cans (14.5 oz. each) diced tomatoes, with juice (not drained)
6 tablespoons chili powder (a blended chili powder mix, not ground chilies)
¼ cup tamari, shoyu, or soy sauce
10 (yes, ten!) medium cloves garlic, minced or pressed
2 tablespoons EACH: agave nectar and balsamic vinegar
2 teaspoons sea salt

1. Heat the oil in a large soup pot over medium-high heat. When the oil is hot, sauté the onions and tempeh in the oil until the onions begin to soften. If necessary, add a little of the broth to prevent sticking.

2. Add everything else (except for the salt) and stir well to combine.

3. Reduce the heat to medium-low and simmer, stirring often, until the mixture is thick and the desired consistency is attained. This should take about 30-45 minutes. Stir in the sea salt and serve.

Serves 8/GF/Green

Calories	Saturated fat (g)	Poly unsat fat (g)	Mono unsat fat (g)	Cholesterol (mg)	Sodium (mg)	Potassium (mg)	Carbohydrate (g)	Dietary fiber (g)	Sugars (g)	Protein (g)
293	1.7	2.7	4.3	0	1980	609	37.9	9	12.9	17.1

Holy Shiitake Lentil Soup

The perfect answer to a rainy day, this delicious soup will lift your spirits, nourish your body, and make your house smell like pure happiness.

1 cup brown lentils
5 cups water
1 cup (packed) sliced shiitake mushroom
  caps
¼ cup "Chicky Baby Seasoning" (p. 16)
1 cup finely chopped kale, stems removed
2 tablespoons balsamic vinegar
1 tablespoon EACH: dried rosemary and
  extra-virgin olive oil
5 large cloves garlic, minced or pressed
1½ teaspoons sea salt

1. Place the lentils, water, shiitakes, and "Chicky Baby Seasoning" in a large pot or pressure cooker. Cover and bring to a boil over high heat. Reduce heat to low and simmer until the lentils are very tender. This will take about 45 minutes in a regular pot or 20 minutes in a pressure cooker.

2. Remove from heat and immediately stir in the remaining ingredients. Once the kale is wilted, serve. This will keep, refrigerated in an airtight container, for a week or so.

Serves 4/GF/SF/Green

	Calories	Saturated fat (g)	Poly unsat fat (g)	Mono unsat fat (g)	Cholesterol (mg)	Sodium (mg)	Potassium (mg)	Carbohydrate (g)	Dietary fiber (g)	Sugars (g)	Protein (g)
HSLS	272	0.7	0.7	2.7	0	1515	750	42.1	17.9	2.5	17.4
15MW	498	1.4	1.4	3.6	0	793	1582	81	30.7	1.1	29.1

15 Minute White Bean and Kale Soup

This soup comes together in a flash and promises to deeply nourish you with every single ingredient.

> Two 15 oz. cans white beans (northern or cannelini), drained and rinsed
> 1 cup lightly packed kale
> 1 cup nondairy milk (plain and unsweetened)
> ¼ cup fresh lemon juice
> 1 tablespoon extra-virgin olive oil
> 3–4 large cloves garlic, pressed or minced
> 1 teaspoon EACH: black pepper, sea salt, dried dill, celery seed, and balsamic vinegar

1. In a blender, combine the beans, kale, and milk until smooth. Transfer to a soup pot.

2. Warm the mixture over medium-low heat. Add the remaining ingredients and stir well. As soon as the mixture is warmed through, remove from heat and serve. This will keep, refrigerated in an airtight container, for about a week.

Serves 3/GF/SF (if using soy-free milk)/Green

Red Lentil Dahl

Yes, this makes a *lot*. But, it's so comforting, light, healthy, and delicious that you'll be happy to have plenty of leftovers! This also freezes well and is delicious plain, over rice, or with warm bread. Yum!

4 cups red lentils
12 cups water
3 cups chopped onions (white or yellow onion)
1 tablespoon EACH: ground cumin and ground coriander
1 teaspoon EACH: asafetida, ground black pepper, and ground turmeric
½ teaspoon ground cayenne

2 tablespoons coconut oil (extra-virgin or regular)
1 cup nondairy milk, plain and unsweetened
¼ cup EACH: fresh lime juice and nutritional yeast
4 teaspoons sea salt

Garnish:
2 cups chopped cilantro

Place the lentils, water, onions, cumin, coriander, asafetida, pepper, turmeric, and cayenne in a very large soup pot. Bring to a boil over high heat. Reduce heat to low and simmer for about 30 minutes, or until the lentils are very tender and mushy.

Stir in the coconut oil until it's melted. Next, stir in the milk, lime juice, yeast, and sea salt. Stir well to thoroughly combine and serve topped with the cilantro.

Serves about 10/GF/SF/Green

Calories	Saturated fat (g)	Poly unsat fat (g)	Mono unsat fat (g)	Cholesterol (mg)	Sodium (mg)	Potassium (mg)	Carbohydrate (g)	Dietary fiber (g)	Sugars (g)	Protein (g)
341	2.6	0.5	0.4	0	922	940	53	25.4	3.9	23.1

Want to do your part to help our furry friends? Each vegan saves the lives of 150-200 animals every year.

Lemon Lover's Red Lentil Spinach Soup

This is my mom's all-time favorite soup—she craves it whenever she's feeling under the weather. With the abundance of cleansing lemon and immune-boosting garlic, it's no wonder!

2 tablespoons plus 2 teaspoons oil
    (sunflower, coconut, olive, or safflower)
Medium-large onion, finely chopped (1½
    cups chopped onion)
6 cups water, preferably filtered
1 cup plus 2 tablespoons dry red lentils
Zest of 1 large organic lemon (about 2
    teaspoons grated or finely minced zest)

It's Thyme for Freshness:
2 teaspoons minced fresh thyme leaves,
    optional
¼ cup plus 2 tablespoons fresh lemon juice
    (start with ¼ cup if you're lemon-shy)
½ cup nondairy milk, plain and unsweetened
4 large cloves garlic, minced or pressed
2 cups (lightly packed) fresh baby spinach
1 tablespoon sea salt (or less if you prefer)
Fresh ground pepper to taste

Green Garnish:
¼ cup minced fresh chives (or scallion tops)

1. In a large soup pot, heat the oil over medium-high heat. Add the onion and sauté for about 10 minutes, stirring often, until soft and lightly browned.

2. Add the water, red lentils, and lemon zest. Cover and bring to a boil. Reduce the heat to low and simmer until the lentils are very soft, about 30-40 minutes.

3. Turn off the heat and add the thyme, lemon juice, milk, garlic, spinach, salt, and pepper. Stir well and cover the soup pot with the lid. Allow the soup to sit, covered, until the spinach is wilted. Stir well and serve garnished with the fresh chives (or scallions). Feel the love.

Serves 6/GF/SF/Green

Calories	Saturated fat (g)	Poly unsat fat (g)	Mono unsat fat (g)	Cholesterol (mg)	Sodium (mg)	Potassium (mg)	Carbohydrate (g)	Dietary fiber (g)	Sugars (g)	Protein (g)
206	5.3	0.3	0.4	0	1146	500	27	12	2.4	10.7

Smoky Split Pea Soup
with Tempeh Bacon Croutons

This simple soup is very nutritious and filling, yet low in calories and fat—perfect for weight loss and glowing health!

Soup:
2¼ cups dry split peas
8 cups water
¼ cup EACH: Chicky Baby Seasoning (p.16) and nutritional yeast
1 tablespoon EACH: balsamic vinegar and liquid smoke
5 large cloves garlic, minced or pressed
2 teaspoons EACH: sea salt, minced or dried rosemary, and black pepper

Tempeh Bacon Croutons:
6 slices tempeh bacon (I use Light Life brand)
2 teaspoons oil (sunflower, coconut, or olive)

1. Place the peas and water in a large pot or pressure cooker. Bring to a boil over high heat. Reduce heat to low and simmer until the peas are completely tender and dissolved. In a pressure cooker, this will take about 20 minutes—in a regular pot, about 40 minutes.

2. Once the peas are done, whisk the mixture with a wire whisk until it's consistent in texture. Whisk in the remaining soup ingredients until thoroughly combined. Set aside.

3. Set a medium skillet over medium heat. Add the oil and tempeh bacon. Cook for 2-3 minutes per side, or until browned on both sides. Remove from heat and break into small pieces.

4. Serve the warm soup topped with the tempeh bacon.

Serves 6/GF/Green

Calories	Saturated fat (g)	Poly unsat fat (g)	Mono unsat fat (g)	Cholesterol (mg)	Sodium (mg)	Potassium (mg)	Carbohydrate (g)	Dietary fiber (g)	Sugars (g)	Protein (g)
345	1.4	0.4	0.3	0	1366	996	54	22.9	7.2	26.4

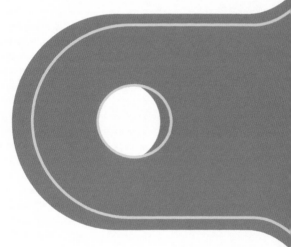

Wraps and Sammies

Here's something I've learned from my clients over the years: So many people depend on wraps and sandwiches, but don't know how to make them in a way that supports weight loss and optimal health. Hence, this chapter! Here, you'll find lots of inspiring recipes that will delight your palate and nourish your body. So, let's wrap things up in a healthy way and enjoy!

Calories	Saturated fat (g)	Poly unsat fat (g)	Mono unsat fat (g)	Cholesterol (mg)	Sodium (mg)	Potassium (mg)	Carbohydrate (g)	Dietary fiber (g)	Sugars (g)	Protein (g)
430	1.2	0.6	0.3	0	986	590	80	10.8	4.9	19.2

Pan Grilled Burrito

This method of making burritos is incredibly user-friendly! Since everything goes right into the tortilla, cleanup is a breeze. Plus, this cooking method turns the tortilla into a crisp, golden brown "crust." Perfection!

One 8-inch sprouted or whole grain flour tortilla (or gluten-free tortilla)
½ cup vegetarian refried beans, black beans, or pinto beans
Optional: ½ cup "Cilantro-Lime Rice" or plain brown rice
2 tablespoons diced onions
¼ cup chopped red cabbage
½ carrot, grated
"Francesca's Salsa" to taste
¼ of a fresh lime (or less if you prefer)

Prepare all of the ingredients you will be using and set them aside. Preheat a dry skillet over medium-low heat.

Place the beans, rice (if using), and onion along the middle of the tortilla. Fold the sides around the filling (as if you were making, say, a burrito). Spray the preheated skillet lightly with oil and place the burrito, seam side down, on the pan. Cover the pan with a lid and cook until the underside is golden-brown. Gently flip it over to cook the other side. If a few fillings try to escape, just tuck them back in the burrito.

When the other side is golden brown as well, remove from the pan. Open the "seam" gently and add the cabbage, carrot, and salsa. Squeeze the fresh lime over the fillings. Close the seam back up to the best of your ability and dig on in.

Serves 1/GF (if using a gluten-free tortilla)/SF/Green

Verde Breakfast Burritos

I enjoy these easy peasy burritos for lunch and dinner too—I just can't get enough of their fresh, vibrant flavor!

2 whole grain tortillas
2/3 cup black beans, warm
2 tablespoons minced onion
2 tablespoons (packed) cilantro, chopped
½ cup salsa verde (tomatillo salsa)
2 teaspoons fresh lime juice

Yellow Potatoes:
1 large baked potato, cold (2 cups chopped potato, cooked and cooled)
1 teaspoon olive oil
1/8 teaspoon turmeric
2 large cloves garlic, minced or pressed
¼ teaspoon sea salt

Prepare all of your ingredients (except the items for the yellow potatoes) and set aside.

In a skillet set to medium heat, heat the chopped potato, olive oil, and turmeric. Gently stir to evenly coat the potatoes with the oil and turmeric. Pan-fry for about 3 minutes, or until the undersides are browned. Flip the pieces over and pan-fry for another 3 minutes, or until both sides are browned and the potatoes are hot.

Place your tortillas in the skillet to warm them (it's OK to put them on top of the potatoes). Fill each tortilla evenly with potatoes, beans, onions, and cilantro. Top with salsa and a drizzle of lime juice. Serve and enjoy!

Serves 2/SF/Green

Cajun Tempeh Wrap

This is one of my favorite go-to entrées. It has it all—big flavor, easy preparation, and loads of nutrients.

Cajun Tempeh:
8 oz. tempeh
2 tablespoons EACH: tamari and fresh lemon juice
2 large cloves garlic, minced or pressed
1 teaspoon olive oil
2 teaspoons Cajun seasoning blend (salt free)

Fixins:
2 whole grain tortillas
2 tablespoons lowfat vegan mayo (such as lowfat Vegenaise)

To taste: Thinly sliced onion, romaine lettuce, shredded carrots, and pickles

Slice the tempeh in half width-wise, then slice it in half again so that the tempeh is half its original thickness. Cut into eight rectangular pieces. Set aside.

Set a medium-large skillet over medium heat and add the oil. Add the tempeh in a single layer. Pour the tamari and lemon juice over the tempeh and turn the tempeh over, so as to coat it evenly with the liquids. Sprinkle the top of the tempeh with one teaspoon of the Cajun seasoning. Cook on one side for about 4 minutes.

Turn the tempeh over and sprinkle with the garlic and remaining Cajun seasoning. Cook for about 4 minutes and then remove from the pan.

To prepare your wraps: Place the tempeh in the tortillas and add the mayo and veggies. Roll up and enjoy!

Serves 2/Green

	Calories	Saturated fat (g)	Poly unsat fat (g)	Mono unsat fat (g)	Cholesterol (mg)	Sodium (mg)	Potassium (mg)	Carbohydrate (g)	Dietary fiber (g)	Sugars (g)	Protein (g)
VBB	520	1.4	0.4	1.7	0	1194	851	95	10.3	6.5	19.7
CTW	603	3.8	5.1	8.6	0	1601	536	71	3.3	1.7	35.2

Zucchini Wraps In No Time

These simple wraps are yet another go-to dish I eat on a regular basis. And why not? They're yummy, quick, high in B vitamins, and very low in calories and fat. Plus, they satisfy my never ending desire for zucchini! This recipes serves one, but you can multiply the amounts for more servings.

2 cups sliced zucchini (sliced into ¼-inch thick rounds, skins on)
1 teaspoon oil (coconut, sunflower, or olive)
1/8 teaspoon EACH: seasoned salt, lemon pepper, and granulated garlic (garlic granules)
1 whole (and/or sprouted) grain tortilla
1 teaspoon nutritional yeast
2 tablespoons minced onion

1. Place a large skillet over medium-high heat and add the oil. Spread out the oil with a spatula, then place the zucchini on the skillet in a single layer (none overlapping). If your skillet isn't large enough, you may need to use an additional skillet or cook the zucchini in two batches.

2. Cook the zucchini for about 4 minutes or until the undersides are golden-browned. Turn the pieces over individually (sorry, I know) and cook another 4 minutes, until both sides are tender and glorious.

3. Sprinkle the zucchini with the seasoned salt, lemon pepper, and garlic and toss well to combine.

4. What I like to do at this point is place my tortilla on top of the zucchini while it's still in the pan—this way the tortilla becomes warm without using another pan. After a few seconds, remove the tortilla and place on a plate. Lay the zucchini down the middle and top with the nutritional yeast and onion. Roll up and enjoy while still warm!

Serves 1/SF/Green

Calories	Saturated fat (g)	Poly unsat fat (g)	Mono unsat fat (g)	Cholesterol (mg)	Sodium (mg)	Potassium (mg)	Carbohydrate (g)	Dietary fiber (g)	Sugars (g)	Protein (g)
396	5.1	0.3	0.3	0	700	677	66	6.3	7.5	16.5

Rainbow Sandwich

The beautiful colors in this sandwich will give you some indication of how vibrantly healthy it is!

    2 slices whole grain (or sprouted grain) bread
    1 tablespoon lowfat vegan mayo (such as
        lowfat Veganaise), optional
    Dijon mustard
    ½ avocado
    ½ yellow tomato, sliced (you can substitute
        red tomato if needed)
    Thinly sliced onion
    ¼ cup peeled, grated beet

Spread one slice of bread with the mayo (if using) and mustard. Mash the avocado on top of that. Add the tomato, onion, and beet. Top with the other slice of bread and enjoy your double rainbow.

    Serves 1/Blue

Thai Green Curry Wrap

This nutritious wrap is flavorful, satisfying, and colorful. What more could you want? Wait, let me get a piece of paper so I can write down your answers.

Thai Green Curry Hummus:
2 cups chickpeas, cooked and drained
¼ cup plus 2 tablespoons fresh lime juice
¼ cup coconut oil
¼ cup fresh basil
¼ cup water
2 teaspoons green curry paste (such as Thai
    Kitchen brand)
1 teaspoon sea salt

Wrap:
5 tortillas (whole grain or sprouted)
1½ cups EACH: grated carrots, chopped red
    cabbage, and baby spinach
To taste: thinly sliced red onion

Place all of the ingredients for the hummus in a food processor or blender. Blend until thoroughly combined, smooth, and creamy. Set aside.

Gently warm the tortillas in a dry skillet. Top evenly with the hummus and vegetables. Roll up and serve immediately.

    Makes 5 wraps/SF/Blue

	Calories	Saturated fat (g)	Poly unsat fat (g)	Mono unsat fat (g)	Cholesterol (mg)	Sodium (mg)	Potassium (mg)	Carbohydrate (g)	Dietary fiber (g)	Sugars (g)	Protein (g)
RS	456	2.2	4.5	13.4	0	528	981	54	12.4	11	13.6
TGCW	531	10.6	1	1	0	1028	420	81	10.3	6.9	18.9

Samosa Wrap with Cilantro Chutney

Samosas as an entrée? Yes, you've officially entered a new dimension, one where your greatest desires have manifested in the form of a tasty sandwich. If you have cooked potatoes on hand, this delicious dish will come together in less than 30 minutes!

Cilantro Chutney:
½ cup (packed) fresh cilantro
1½ tablespoons finely shredded coconut
1 tablespoon EACH: chopped fresh ginger and dry-roasted peanuts
2 small-medium cloves garlic, peeled
½ small jalapeno, seeded (or less if you prefer your chutney less spicy)
½ teaspoon cumin seeds
¼ teaspoon sea salt
1 tablespoon fresh lime juice
¼ cup water

Samosa Filling:
2 teaspoons oil (sunflower, non-virgin olive, or coconut)
1 teaspoon EACH: brown mustard seeds and cumin seeds
1 teaspoon EACH: ground cumin and ground coriander
½ teaspoon ground turmeric
1/8 teaspoon ground cayenne
3 cups chopped cooked potato (skins on and cut into small cubes)
2 tablespoons fresh lemon juice
2 large cloves garlic, minced or pressed
½ cup green peas (frozen or fresh)
½ teaspoon sea salt

Wrapping Things Up:
4 whole grain tortillas
2 teaspoons oil (sunflower, non-virgin olive, or coconut)
½ teaspoon cumin seeds

1. First, get your chutney on. In a food processor or blender, place all of the chutney ingredients. Blend well until the mixture is thoroughly combined – you will want to retain a little texture, but not too much!

2. Preheat your oven to 400 F. In a large skillet or wok, add the oil, mustard seeds, and cumin seeds and place over medium heat. Stir-fry for a minute, then add the cumin, coriander, turmeric, and cayenne. Stir-fry for another few seconds until the spices become aromatic. Then add the potatoes and stir well until the potatoes are evenly coated with the spices.

3. Add the lemon juice, garlic, peas, and sea salt to the potato mixture. Stir well and remove from heat.

4. Place the tortillas on a flat surface and place the potato mixture evenly in the center of each tortilla. Fold the sides in, then roll up from the bottom so that you have enclosed wraps.

5. Brush the wraps with the remaining 2 teaspoons oil and sprinkle with the ½ teaspoon cumin seeds. Bake for about 20 minutes (turning over halfway through), or until golden-browned and crisp.

6. To serve, cut each wrap in half and serve with the chutney.

Serves 4/SF/Green

Calories	Saturated fat (g)	Poly unsat fat (g)	Mono unsat fat (g)	Cholesterol (mg)	Sodium (mg)	Potassium (mg)	Carbohydrate (g)	Dietary fiber (g)	Sugars (g)	Protein (g)
495	5.7	0.7	1.2	0	871	603	86	6.9	3.7	16.6

Christina's Tempeh Burger Wraps

Back in our college days, I'd visit my good friend Christina's cute little apartment and we would eat these wraps, leave silly outgoing messages on her answering machine, and laugh until our sides ached. I still think of that every time I eat these—which is often, considering how quick and yummy they are!

8 oz. tempeh (any kind of plain tempeh such as five-grain, wild rice, or soy)
1 teaspoon olive oil
2 tablespoons tamari
3 large garlic cloves, minced or pressed

3 whole grain tortillas

To taste:
Yellow mustard, ketchup, chopped dill pickles, sliced onions, and lettuce

Slice the tempeh in half to open the package, then into ½-inch by 2-inch strips.

Set a medium skillet over medium-high heat and add the oil.

Add the tempeh to the skillet in a single layer. Pour the tamari on top and sprinkle with the garlic. Turn the tempeh to evenly coat with the oil, tamari, and garlic. Cook for about 2-3 minutes, then flip and cook for another 2-3 minutes, or until the tempeh is browned on both sides. Remove from heat.

Gently heat your tortillas (personally, I just place them on top of the skillet over the tempeh for about 30 seconds). Fill each tortilla with tempeh and add the mustard, ketchup, pickles, onions, and lettuce. Roll up and enjoy.

Serves 3/Green

Spicy Indian Wraps

Yet another reason to live.

Spicy Onion Chutney:
¾ cup plus 1 tablespoon very finely diced onion (yellow or white)
1 tablespoon fresh lemon juice
1 teaspoon EACH: oil (sunflower, melted coconut, or non-virgin olive), paprika, and ketchup
¼ teaspoon EACH: sea salt, cumin powder, cayenne powder, and coriander powder

Potato Mixture:
1½ cups chopped potatoes (cooked, cooled potatoes, cut into ½-inch thick cubes)
1 teaspoon oil (sunflower, non-virgin olive, or coconut)
1 teaspoon cumin seeds
1 teaspoon ground coriander
½ teaspoon EACH: sea salt and ground turmeric
1 tablespoon fresh lemon juice

3 tortillas, whole or sprouted grain
One 15 oz. can black-eyed peas, drained and rinsed (1½ cups cooked beans)
¾ cup finely chopped cabbage, red or green

1. In a small bowl, place all of the "Spicy Onion Chutney" ingredients. Stir well and set aside.

2. Heat a medium skillet over medium-high heat. Add the potatoes, oil, and cumin seeds. Stir well and cook for one minute. Next, add the coriander, sea salt, and turmeric. Stir well and cook for another 3-4 minutes, or until the potatoes are browned and crisp. Sprinkle with the lemon juice and set aside.

3. To assemble: Gently warm your tortillas. Place the following along the center of each tortilla: ¼ cup of cabbage, ¼ cup chutney, ½ cup of black-eyed peas, and a third of the potato mixture. Roll up and enjoy!

Serves 3/SF/Green

	Calories	Saturated fat (g)	Poly unsat fat (g)	Mono unsat fat (g)	Cholesterol (mg)	Sodium (mg)	Potassium (mg)	Carbohydrate (g)	Dietary fiber (g)	Sugars (g)	Protein (g)
CTBW	471	2.9	3.1	3.4	0	1118	349	65	3.2	1.2	27.5
SIW	614	3.9	0.5	0.4	0	1030	966	113	18.5	4.8	27.1

Vegan Meatball Wrap and You'll Never Go Back

Once you take a bite out of this insanely scrumptious creation, you'll never crave an animal-based meatball sandwich again! But be warned—it's messy. The sort of thing you'd save for a third date, after your potential life partner thinks you're cute with marinara on your chin.

Banzoballs:
2 tablespoons EACH: water and tamari
1 cup cooked garbanzo beans (chickpeas)
½ cup EACH: breadcrumbs (from whole grain bread) and vital wheat gluten
2 tablespoons extra-virgin olive oil
½ teaspoon EACH (dried): rosemary, basil, sage, oregano, and apple cider vinegar
3 cloves garlic, minced or pressed

Mushrooms:
3 cups sliced baby portabella mushrooms
1 teaspoon EACH: olive oil and tamari
½ teaspoon balsamic vinegar
2 large cloves garlic, minced or pressed

Wrap It Up:
3 whole grain tortillas
½ cup shredded vegan mozzarella cheese (such as Daiya)
1½ cups vegan marinara sauce, heated until hot
¼ cup EACH: minced onions and sliced pepperoncini
3 tablespoons fresh basil, cut into ribbons

To make the banzoballs: Preheat your oven to 400 F. Blend the water, tamari, and chickpeas in a food processor or blender until smooth. Remove to a large bowl.

Add the remaining banzoball ingredients (breadcrumbs, gluten, oil, herbs, vinegar, and garlic) to the bean mixture and stir well to combine. Once well combined, knead for a minute or two (either in the bowl or on your countertop). Form into 1-inch balls and place on a lightly oiled baking sheet.

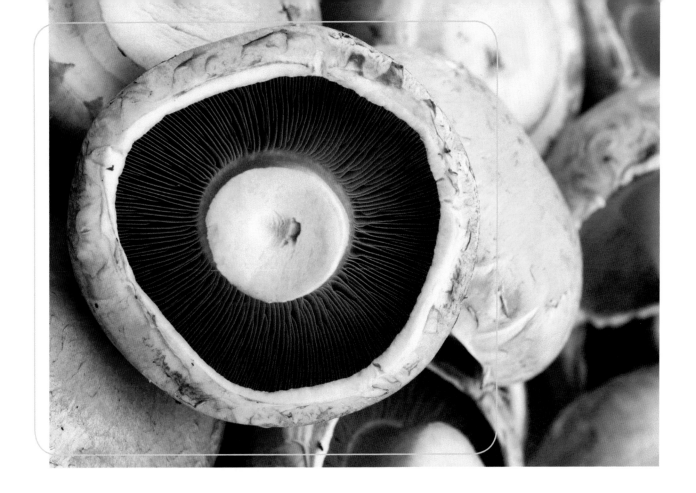

Bake the banzoballs for 10-15 minutes, or until browned on the bottom. Remove and turn over. Bake for another 10-15 minutes, or until the balls are nicely browned on both sides. Set aside.

To make the mushrooms: Place the mushrooms, oil, tamari, and garlic in a medium skillet over medium-high heat. Sauté for about 5 minutes, stirring often, until the mushrooms are tender and browned. Set aside.

To finish your delicious creations: Warm the tortillas in a dry skillet or oven. Place the cheese down the center of each tortilla and immediately top with the hot marinara so as to help the cheese melt. Top evenly with the banzo balls and add the mushrooms, onions, pepperoncini, and basil to each wrap. Fold up and get your fix!

Makes 3 wraps/Blue

Calories	Saturated fat (g)	Poly unsat fat (g)	Mono unsat fat (g)	Cholesterol (mg)	Sodium (mg)	Potassium (mg)	Carbohydrate (g)	Dietary fiber (g)	Sugars (g)	Protein (g)
811	4.9	2.5	8.3	0	2470	615	110	13.6	8.9	40.8

Greek Hummus Wraps

These fresh, flavorful wraps are especially easy to make if you keep the hummus and veggies prepared in the fridge. Then, it only takes about two minutes to roll up some lunch!

One recipe "Lowfat Supercharged Hummus" (p. 25)

3 whole grain or sprouted tortillas
¾ cup diced cucumber
1 cup fresh spinach
¼ cup fresh basil, thinly sliced
1 medium tomato, diced
2 tablespoons kalamata olives, pitted

Gently warm the tortillas in a dry pan.

Spread them evenly with the hummus and evenly place the remaining ingredients down the center. Roll up and enjoy!

Serves 3/Green

Calories	Saturated fat (g)	Poly unsat fat (g)	Mono unsat fat (g)	Cholesterol (mg)	Sodium (mg)	Potassium (mg)	Carbohydrate (g)	Dietary fiber (g)	Sugars (g)	Protein (g)
635	2.2	2.4	4.3	0	1092	783	104	16.8	10.4	29.5

BBQ Tempeh Wraps

This delicious entrée is a great introduction to tempeh for those who've never tried it. Tempeh is a nutrient-dense whole food, made from fermented soy and other grains. It's very high in fiber and is immune-boosting and great for your digestion. Viva la tempeh!

8 oz. tempeh, cut into ½-inch cubes
¼ cup water
1 tablespoon tamari
1 cup prepared barbeque sauce (a natural, vegan brand such as Annie's)

3 tortillas, whole grain or sprouted

Your choice of fixings:
Lowfat vegan mayo (such as Veganaise)
Pickles, lettuce, thinly sliced onion, shredded cabbage, grated carrots

1. Preheat your oven to 375 F.

2. Place the tempeh in a medium pan set to medium-high heat. Evenly pour the tamari over the tempeh and stir. Pour the water on top and cook the mixture, stirring occasionally, until all of the liquids have been absorbed. Remove from heat and set aside.

3. Spread a layer of the barbeque sauce on the bottom of a small baking pan (about the size of a pie pan). Put the tempeh on top of the sauce and cover the tempeh with the remaining 1 cup of sauce. Bake for 15 minutes. Remove from the oven, stir, and place back in the oven for another 15 minutes. Remove and stir again. Bake for a final 10-15 minutes (for a total of 40-45 minutes), or until the tempeh is very gooey and the sauce is really thick. Remove from the oven.

4. Gently warm the tortillas in a dry pan and place on plates. Evenly distribute the tempeh down the middle of each tortilla and add your choice of fixings. Roll up and enjoy.

Serves 3/Green

Calories	Saturated fat (g)	Poly unsat fat (g)	Mono unsat fat (g)	Cholesterol (mg)	Sodium (mg)	Potassium (mg)	Carbohydrate (g)	Dietary fiber (g)	Sugars (g)	Protein (g)
585	2.7	2.9	2.3	0	1490	324	91	3.1	20.1	26.6

Sweet and Spicy Tempeh Sandwich

This sandwich is very easy to make and deliciously addictive as well! But you won't find me on street corners selling them—not anymore. Not since the arrest.

Sweet and Spicy Tempeh
8 oz. tempeh
¼ cup water
2 tablespoons tamari
2 tablespoons maple syrup
2 teaspoons toasted sesame oil
½ teaspoon sriracha sauce (use more if you like more heat—I use a full teaspoon)
3 large cloves garlic

Sammy:
4 sliced whole or sprouted grain bread
2 tablespoons lowfat vegan mayo (such as reduced fat Vegenaise)
To taste: lettuce, thinly sliced onions, pickles

Slice the tempeh in half (width-wise) and then slice it in half again so that each slab is half its original thickness and length. Place the tempeh in a medium skillet along with the water. Steam the tempeh on medium-high heat until the water has evaporated.

Pour the tamari, maple syrup, toasted sesame oil over the tempeh and turn over to coat both sides. Spread with the sriracha sauce and garlic. Cook over medium-high heat for about 3 minutes on each side, or until both sides are gloriously caramelized looking. Remove from heat and set aside.

To make up your sandwich, toast the bread if you like and then spread two slices (one for each sandwich) with the mayo. Add the lettuce, onions, and pickles to each sandwich. Finally, place the tempeh on the vegetables and top with the remaining bread. Cut each sandwich in half and serve.

Serves 2/Blue

Calories	Saturated fat (g)	Poly unsat fat (g)	Mono unsat fat (g)	Cholesterol (mg)	Sodium (mg)	Potassium (mg)	Carbohydrate (g)	Dietary fiber (g)	Sugars (g)	Protein (g)
596	3.2	8.8	8.7	0	1516	674	66	4.2	20.7	33.2

Chili Lime Tempeh Fajitas

These filling wraps are delicious, immune-boosting, and very nutrient-dense. For a "Green" entrée, you can omit the guacamole and squeeze a little extra lime on top.

Chili Lime Tempeh:
8 oz. tempeh
2 tablespoons plus 1 tablespoon fresh lime juice
1 tablespoon tamari
1 teaspoon minced lime zest (the zest of one large lime)
3 large cloves garlic, minced or pressed
¼ teaspoon ground cayenne
1 teaspoon olive oil
¼ teaspoon sea salt

Guacamole:
1 avocado, ripe and ready
1 tablespoon EACH: fresh lime juice and minced fresh cilantro
1 medium clove garlic, minced or pressed
⅛ teaspoon sea salt

Wraps:
2 whole grain tortillas
1 cup red cabbage, finely chopped
½ cup chopped cilantro
¼ cup thinly sliced onion

Begin by marinating the tempeh: Cut the tempeh into small rectangular strips so that you have about 32 pieces of tempeh. Place on a large plate. Pour the 2 tablespoons of lime juice and tamari over the tempeh. Sprinkle with the zest, garlic, and cayenne. Set aside for about ten minutes. Flip the pieces over and marinate until all of the liquid is absorbed.

Meanwhile, make the guacamole: Remove the avocado flesh from its skin and place it in a bowl. Mash it very well with a fork. Stir in the lime juice, cilantro, garlic, and salt until very well combined. Set aside.

Set a medium pan over medium heat and add the teaspoon of oil. Pan-fry the tempeh for 2-3 minutes on each side, or until it is nicely browned. Remove from heat and toss with the remaining tablespoon of lime juice. Sprinkle with the ¼ teaspoon sea salt and set aside.

Warm the tortillas gently in a dry pan. Place the tempeh along the center of the tortillas, along with the guacamole and vegetables. Roll up and enjoy!

Serves 2/Blue

Calories	Saturated fat (g)	Poly unsat fat (g)	Mono unsat fat (g)	Cholesterol (mg)	Sodium (mg)	Potassium (mg)	Carbohydrate (g)	Dietary fiber (g)	Sugars (g)	Protein (g)
740	6	6.5	14.9	0	1391	1151	85	11.6	4.3	37.3

Chicky Burgers

These savory burgers are extremely easy to make, especially if you've gotten into the habit of keeping the Chicky Baby Seasoning on hand.

1½ cups cooked garbanzo beans (chickpeas)
¼ cup water
½ cup EACH: grated carrots and rolled oats
¼ cup Chicky Baby Seasoning (p. 16)
2 tablespoons fresh lemon juice
1 tablespoon extra-virgin olive oil
3 large cloves garlic, minced or pressed
½ teaspoon sea salt
½ cup vital wheat gluten

Fixins:
5 whole grain burger buns
¼ cup lowfat vegan mayo (such as Vegenaise reduced fat mayonnaise)
To taste: Yellow mustard, thinly sliced onions, pickles, lettuce, tomato slices

Place the garbanzo beans and water in a food processor and blend until smooth. Remove to a medium-sized bowl.

Stir the carrots, oats, seasoning, lemon juice, oil, garlic, and salt into the mixture until thoroughly combined. Lastly, stir in the gluten. Use your hands to work the gluten in, then knead the mixture for a minute or so.

Form the mixture into large balls, then form into patties. Lightly oil or spray a large skillet set to medium-high heat. Pan-fry the patties for about 3-5 minutes per side, or until the patties are golden-browned on each side.

Remove from heat and assemble your sandwich: Spread the burger buns with the mayo and mustard and top with the onions, pickles, lettuce, tomato, and a burger patty.

Serves 5/Green

Calories	Saturated fat (g)	Poly unsat fat (g)	Mono unsat fat (g)	Cholesterol (mg)	Sodium (mg)	Potassium (mg)	Carbohydrate (g)	Dietary fiber (g)	Sugars (g)	Protein (g)
361	1.3	2.1	6.5	0	1030	415	45.4	8	6	21.7

Chipotle Lime Beanoa Burgers

This is my newest go-to burger recipe—I just can't get enough of the smoky lime flavor and nutrient-dense goodness. Plus, you can get the entire recipe together in under 20 minutes! I personally love these so much that I usually eat them just plain! However, they're great in a bun with all the fixin's too.

Note: The name "beanoa" is my take on the cross between beans and quinoa, so you'd say it like this: "bean-wah."

15 oz. can black beans, drained
2 cups cooked quinoa
1 cup quick-cooking rolled oats (the quick-cooking variety works best here)
½ cup finely grated carrot
2 tablespoons fresh lime juice
1 tablespoon minced lime zest (the zest of two medium limes)
4 large cloves garlic, minced or pressed
1 teaspoon sea salt
½ teaspoon ground chipotle powder

Optional, for serving:
Whole grain buns
Lettuce, tomato, sliced onions, pickles, ketchup, mustard, lowfat vegan mayo

Place the drained black beans in a bowl. Mash them well with a potato masher or fork. They should be very well mashed, but not completely smooth. There's a reason we're not just throwing them in a blender.

Stir the remaining ingredients into the beans until thoroughly combined.

Heat a large skillet over medium-high heat and spray lightly with oil.

To make the burgers: Remove the mixture in ½-cup increments and form into circular patties. Place on the hot skillet and pan-fry for about 3-4 minutes. Flip the patties over and cook another 3-4 minutes, or until both sides are lightly browned. Remove to a plate. You may need to cook these in two or three batches, depending on the size of your skillet.

To serve: You can be a rebel like me and just savor them plain, or serve them on buns with your choice of fixin's. Any leftover burgers can be stored in the fridge (in an airtight container) for several days, or frozen for several weeks or more.

Makes 7 burgers/GF (with gluten-free oats and buns)/SF/Green

Calories	Saturated fat (g)	Poly unsat fat (g)	Mono unsat fat (g)	Cholesterol (mg)	Sodium (mg)	Potassium (mg)	Carbohydrate (g)	Dietary fiber (g)	Sugars (g)	Protein (g)
197	0.2	0.5	0.3	0	331	390	35.9	8.5	0.7	9.5

Acknowledgments

We are so very thankful to all of the lovely people who made this book possible. For starters, our photographers are unsung heroes! Olga Vasiljeva and Janet Malowany worked incredibly hard to snap their gorgeous photos for us, despite an inconveniently short deadline. Thank you so, so, so much, you amazing ladies! Also, thanks to Michelle Bebber for letting us use some of your beautiful photos as well. You are so talented and generous!

Thanks to Heather Shaw for creating a gorgeous layout for our book. You took it from blah to BAM! We are thrilled with our book, and it's largely because of all of your hard work, creative genius, and long hours. We just hope you want to keep designing our books because you're irreplaceable!

We are also grateful to our dedicated **Get Waisted** directors. You know who you are, and you are all incredible! We appreciate your hard work, enthusiasm, and commitment to the Get Waisted program. Thank you for spreading the word and helping us turn the health of this country around—one person at a time. We love each and every one of you!

Thanks to our assistant Stacia (Stacey) for her attention to detail, creative thinking, intelligence, and integrity. You're just too wonderful for words and we're so lucky to have you!

Our families also inspire us. Tess's daughter Alethea and her husband Carl are the definition of love and support. Thank you both for being ridiculously awesome.

Mary wants to thank Mark for inspiration, and Anna and Chelsea for support and all of their love—and without Mary's mom, the book would still be languishing in a drawer untitled. Mary also wants to thank her friend Anne Stanton, without whom we'd all be Waisters instead of **Get Waisted**!

And finally, thanks to you—our readers and fans. Each of you means more to us than you know. We would truly be nowhere without you! You are beautiful and you are deeply appreciated.

Thank you, thank you, thank you!

Index

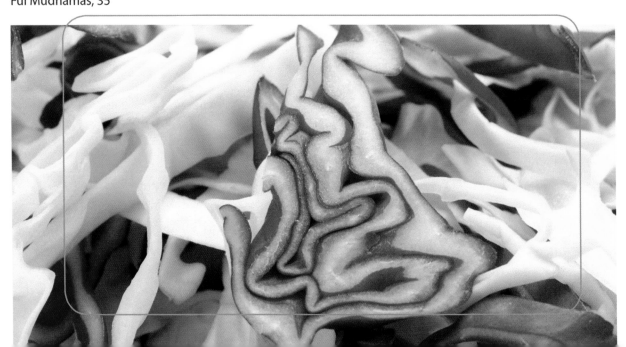

Many thanks to our wonderful photographers!

Photographs by Olga Vasiljeva: Ever So Nice Beans and Rice, Hungarian Chickpeas, Savory Lentils with Caramelized Onions, Moroccan French Lentils, Orange Ginger Veggie Noodle Bowl, Lemon Ginger Miso Noodles, Nori Rolls with Lemon-Lime Soy Dipping Sauce, Pineapple Rice, Double Garlic Quinoa, Cheesy Broccoli Baked Potato, Rosemary Polenta with Mushrooms, Get Skinny Soup, Hearty Vegan Chili, 15 Minute White Bean and Kale Soup, Zucchini Wraps In No Time, and Greek Hummus Wraps

Photographs by Janet Malowany: Black-eyed Peas with Kale, Black Bean and Rice Bowl with Mango Salsa, Mung Beans with Cilantro Chutney, Japanese Ume Rice, Lemon Asparagus Quinoa, and Red Lentil Dahl

Photographs by Michelle Bebber: Creamy Adzuki Beans, Perfect Pasta, Cilantro Lime Rice, and Lemon Lover's Red Lentil Spinach Soup

Made in the USA
Lexington, KY
18 June 2014